MW01626240

From Cotton to Countdown

A Culinary Celebration of Southern Tradition

Ladies Association of Madison Academy

FROM COTTON TO COUNTDOWN
A CULINARY CELEBRATION OF SOUTHERN TRADITION

Published by
Ladies Association of Madison Academy

Copyright © 2009 by
Ladies Association of Madison Academy
325 Slaughter Road
Madison, Alabama 35758
256-971-1619

Cover Photograph: King Cotton © 1907 by J. C. Coovert
Photograph on page 5 by Kimberly S. Whitaker
Photographs on pages 10, 30, 42, 58, 72, 84, 106, and 151
courtesy of the Huntsville Madison County Public Library
Photograph on page 122 courtesy NASA
Photograph on page 160 © by Lee Milam

This cookbook is a collection of favorite recipes,
which are not necessarily original recipes.

All rights reserved. No part of this publication may be reproduced in any form or by any means, electronic or mechanical, including photocopying and recording, or by any information storage or retrieval system, without prior written permission from Ladies Association of Madison Academy.

ISBN: 978-0-9815748-0-6

Edited, Designed, and Produced by

CommunityClassics™

an imprint of

a wholly owned subsidiary of
Southwestern/Great American, Inc.

P.O. Box 305142
Nashville, Tennessee 37230
800-358-0560

Manufactured in the United States of America
First Printing: 2009
4,000 copies

Ladies Association of Madison Academy

LAMA is a group of ladies who share in the desire of making positive educational differences in the lives of our children, grandchildren, and others. We share our time, efforts, and resources to provide services and educational improvements for the children of Madison Academy. We believe that LAMA and Christian education foster a spirit of friendship and fellowship between its members and encourages the development of spiritual and social values between its members and their families.

Mission Statement

Our mission for this cookbook was to assemble a collection of classic southern recipes and reflect on hospitality from the Tennessee Valley. The proceeds from this book will provide support for the ongoing educational endeavors of Madison Academy, a K-12 Christian school located in Huntsville, Alabama.

Dedication

There are so many decisions to be made when editing a cookbook. What is our book theme and what will go on the cover? To whom will the book be dedicated? How many recipes can we use? Which pound cake recipe is best? The list goes on and on!

While all of these important issues were being discussed, the question of book dedication was very easy. There was only one logical person.

Margie Smith, or "Sarge Marge" as we all lovingly call her, was our obvious choice.

Where does one begin to describe Sarge?

Sarge Marge is first and foremost an educator. She has taught most everyone south of the Mason-Dixon line! (If she didn't teach you, she taught your momma or daddy, aunt or uncle, or third-cousin twice-removed!) In other words, Sarge NEVER meets a stranger. Actually, you might THINK you don't know her, but do not be fooled—I am sure she knows you AND your people!

She is a school administrator, tour guide, Sunday school teacher, and mentor; a member of heaven only knows how many civic clubs; a loving wife and mother, grandmother, and friend to thousands. She has worn all of these hats at the same time, usually juggling more things in one day than humanly possible!

It is no secret to many that the doors of Madison Academy would have closed many years ago without her perseverance and dedication. She is and always will be MA's matriarch and mascot. She is irreplaceable!

Now don't get me wrong! Sarge is not perfect. Some might even say she can get a little bossy! She has even been known to get herself in a pickle or two along the way. But even in a pickle, she comes out smelling like a rose and has everyone's best interest at heart!

Maybe it's her imperfections we love the most. Some of her claims to fame are, as we call them, her "Margie-isms." She has a tendency to get so busy in the moment that she may mispronounce a word or two. Most of her "Margie-isms" seem to occur when she's on a tour bus (that's motor coach in Sarge language) with fifty kids and parents—so who could blame her! When corrected, she's always a great sport and is never too proud to laugh at herself.

We hope you will enjoy some of her words and stories scattered throughout the book in recipe titles. We just couldn't pass up the chance to print some of them! They're good for a chuckle, even if you don't know her from Adam's housecat! If you haven't been fortunate enough to have met Sarge, we hope our book will give you insight into a very special, one-of-a-kind lady. We encourage you to come over to the school sometime and try to catch her. She will be the blur you see whizzing by—if she isn't off touring on a motor coach!

Sarge, we couldn't love you more. You brighten our days with love, learning, and laughter. This book is respectfully dedicated to you in honor of your many years of service to both Madison Academy and the Huntsville community . . . and shall we even say . . . the south!

May your life continue to be filled with the joy of knowing how many people will never be the same . . . because of you.

KIMBERLY S. WHITAKER

Happy traveling
Happy cooking
Love, Sarge

Table of Contents

Acknowledgments

Carol Brittain
Margaret Clouser
Covington's Downtowne Luncheon Café and Catering Company
Wendy Green
Huntsville Madison County Public Library
Kenny Dodson of Kenny Mango's Coffee Shop
Lee Milam
Katherine Riggins
Margie Smith
Southerland's Photography
Malcolm Tarkington
The Development Office of Madison Academy

Committee Members

Project Editor

Kimberly S. Whitaker

Editorial Team and Copy Editors

Anissa Benson
Beth Flatt
Lane Hamric
Lisa Mayes

Archivist and Historical Consultant

Raneé G. Pruitt

Art Direction

Lee Milam
Kimberly S. Whitaker

Marketing Consultants

Kristal Huntley
Shirley Trillio

Assistant Copy Writer

David N. Hall

Recipe Testers

Anissa Benson
Dianne Brackin
Ann Clark
Teresa DeVore
Beth Flatt
Paula Hamlett
Lane Hamric
Cara Hargett
Lisa Mayes
Carolyn E. Moses
Kristy Palmer
Kathy Passon
Sue Passon
Cindy Richardson
Gloria Scherzinger
Amy Sides
Margie Smith
Kimberly S. Whitaker
Donna Wicks
Lisa Yokley

INTRODUCTION

To understand the title **From Cotton to Countdown**, *one would have to learn a bit about Huntsville's emergence into the sophisticated southern city it has become today.*

Huntsville's settlement period began with Tennessean John Hunt, who ventured down to the area with a friend named Bean. The two men stopped and spent the night with the Criner family on the banks of the Flint River, where Mrs. Criner welcomed them with a hearty Scotch-Irish meal. The next morning, Hunt went on to stake his claim on the Big Spring. From 1805 Huntsville continued to grow and boast of many successes before the Civil War. One such success was having one of the first public water systems. Huntsville served as the first capital of Alabama in 1819, and as an early nineteenth-century center for banking and business. Huntsville and its surrounding areas developed a strong cotton-based economy, which also strengthened the extensive cotton market.

After the Civil War, Huntsville rapidly made plans to make the city more appealing to large-scale industrial developers. This progressive way of thinking introduced a group of businessmen called the North Alabama Improvement Company. They spearheaded a campaign to bring the cotton mills to the cotton fields, and ventured deep into textile production, rather than to keep sending raw cotton to the north, where factories there would turn raw cotton into material. In 1891, Dallas Manufacturing opened, and its 25,000 spindles rivaled the great factories of the already industrialized north. The age of industrialization had been embraced by the area, and other large-scale textile companies followed in making Huntsville their home. One such industrial giant was Merrimack Manufacturing of Lowell, Massachusetts. Huntsville's textile industry transformed basic cotton picking into full-scale production, which shipped a portion of its products to China, thus making Huntsville not only a leading city of the south, but also internationally. Some of its proud citizens hailed their beloved city as "Queen City of the South."

Textile production suffered great losses during the Depression, and Huntsville wisely looked to new and inventive ways of improving the city's potential. Our leaders promoted north Alabama and its beautiful Tennessee Valley, touting its ideal environment for agriculture, education, industry, and the arts. Once again, Huntsville was preparing for rapid growth.

During World War II, the United States government chose Huntsville as a site for munitions factories, and Redstone Arsenal was born. Shortly thereafter, in 1950, Wernher von Braun and his team of German scientists moved to Huntsville to facilitate missile research and production. It wouldn't be long until brilliant teams of engineers and scientists would converge on Huntsville, placing it on the global map in research and space development.

The cotton market town of the past began to fade and a great center of technology and commerce emerged into the thriving Huntsville we know and enjoy today. Although many of our cotton-covered fields have now been replaced by towering buildings, Huntsville will never forget its deep roots and rich heritage, which grew from a tiny white blossom.

RANEÉ G. PRUITT

"King Cotton"

In 1808, Madison County was officially created by proclamation of the Governor of the Mississippi Territory. A rapid influx of settlers started arriving and clearing the fields. Within eight years, Madison County was producing more than ten thousand bales of cotton for the market, doubling the production of cotton in any other county of its size in the States. One thousand pounds of cotton per acre could be consistently harvested by the farmers of Madison County. The high cotton price was the financial backbone of the prospering city of Huntsville, and the west side of the public square eventually became known as "Cotton Row." Area farmers brought their cotton by cart and wagon to merchants on the square to be sold and then it shipped to New Orleans. Huntsville was so dependent on cotton that the entire west side of the square was reserved for cotton wagons.

Just as King Cotton was a mainstay to this area, so were some of the traditional Southern favorites found within this chapter. Some might have been scribbled on an index card and tucked into a tattered apron pocket, long since misplaced. Most, however, have gone unwritten, only to be found in the memories of our "dearly departed." Hopefully these classics will not only be useful, but will evoke memories of simpler times spent around kitchen tables throughout the South.

Deep Roots

Traditional Southern Classics

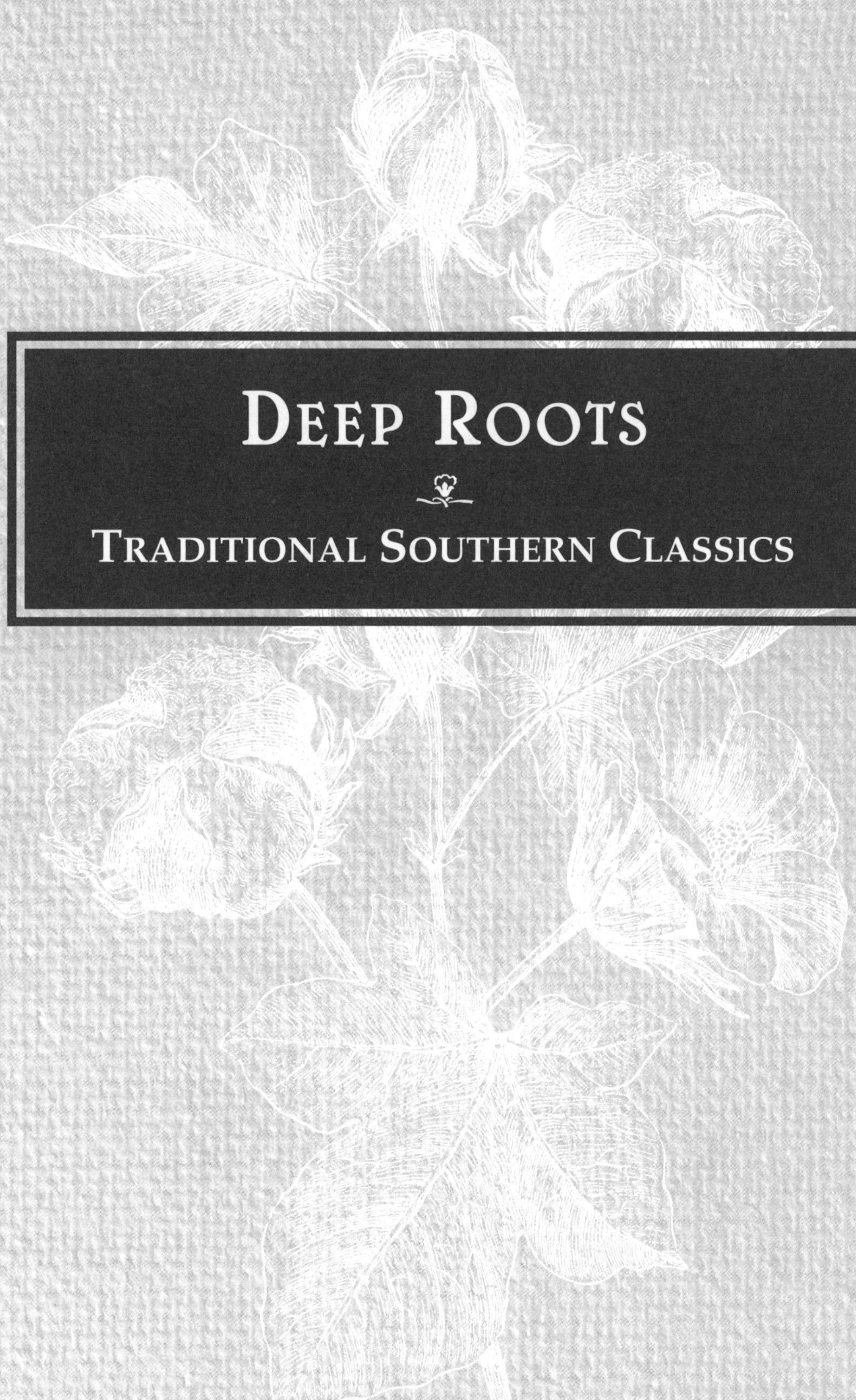

Bama Boys Meat Loaf

1 (8-ounce) can tomato sauce
1/4 cup packed brown sugar
1/4 cup white vinegar
1 teaspoon prepared mustard
2 pounds ground chuck
1 onion, minced
1/4 cup crushed crackers
1 egg, lightly beaten
$1^1/2$ teaspoons salt
1/4 teaspoon pepper
1/4 teaspoon Accent

Mix the tomato sauce, brown sugar, vinegar and mustard in a saucepan. Bring to a boil. Reduce the heat and keep warm. Combine the ground chuck, onion, crackers, egg, salt, pepper and Accent in a bowl and mix well. Shape into a loaf and place in a baking dish. Pour the sauce over the top. Bake at 350 degrees for 1 hour.

Serves 6 to 8

Regal Roast Beef

1 ($5^1/2$- to 6-pound) beef rump roast
1 tablespoon Kitchen Bouquet browning and seasoning sauce
Seasoned salt to taste
Lemon pepper to taste
Garlic powder to taste
1 onion, thinly sliced
1 cup red wine
$1^1/2$ tablespoons cornstarch
1 cup cold water

Line a heavy roasting pan with heavy-duty foil sprayed with nonstick cooking spray, allowing extra foil to hang over the edges.

Brush the roast with the browning and seasoning sauce. Sprinkle generously with seasoned salt, lemon pepper and garlic powder. Place half the onion in a cast-iron Dutch oven or deep heavy ovenproof skillet. Place the roast fat side up on top of the onion. Top with the remaining onion. Bake, uncovered, at 400 degrees for 30 minutes. Reduce the oven temperature to 325 degrees. Pour the wine over the roast and cover with a tight-fitting lid. Bake for 3 hours. Let stand before slicing.

Remove the pan juices to a saucepan and skim the surface. Dissolve the cornstarch in the water in a bowl. Stir into the pan juices. Cook until thick and bubbly, stirring constantly. Serve with the sliced beef.

Serves 6 to 8

Five-Hour Beef Stew

2 pounds beef cubes
1 (12-ounce) package baby carrots
4 potatoes, chopped
1 onion, sliced into rings
3 tablespoons instant tapioca granules
1 tablespoon sugar
3 cups vegetable juice cocktail
Salt and pepper to taste

Combine the beef, carrots, potatoes, onion, tapioca granules, sugar and vegetable juice cocktail in a roasting pan and mix well. Season with salt and pepper. Toss until combined. Bake, covered, at 250 degrees for 5 hours. Do not open the oven while cooking.

Serves 6

Comfort Noodle Soup

4 cups chicken broth
4 cups water
10 chicken bouillon cubes
4 cups uncooked medium egg noodles
2 (10-ounce) cans cream of chicken soup
3 cups shredded cooked chicken breast
2 teaspoons pepper
1½ cups sour cream
1 bunch parsley, finely chopped

Combine the broth, water and bouillon cubes in a large saucepan or stockpot and bring to a boil. Boil for 5 minutes. Reduce the heat to low and stir in the noodles. Cook for 10 minutes. Stir in the soup, chicken and pepper. Cook until heated through. Stir in the sour cream just before serving. Ladle into bowls and sprinkle each serving with some of the parsley.

Serves 15 to 20

Low-Fat Chicken and Dumplings

4 boneless skinless chicken breasts
4 cups chicken broth, or 1 tablespoon chicken base
Salt and pepper to taste
2 (10-ounce) cans cream of chicken soup
1 (10-count) package 10-inch flour tortillas

Combine the chicken and broth in a large saucepan. Season with salt and pepper. Bring to a boil and boil until the chicken is cooked through and tender. Remove the chicken to a bowl and shred. Return the cooking liquid to a boil and stir in the soup. Slice the tortillas into 1-inch-wide strips. Add gradually to the boiling liquid. Stir in the chicken. Reduce the heat to low and simmer for 5 to 10 minutes, stirring occasionally.

Serves 6 to 8

Poppy Seed Chicken

8 chicken breasts, cooked and chopped
2 (10-ounce) cans cream of chicken soup
1 cup sour cream
2 cups crushed Ritz crackers
3 tablespoons poppy seeds
1/2 cup (1 stick) margarine, melted

Spread the chicken in a buttered 9×13-inch baking dish. Combine the soup and sour cream in a saucepan. Cook until heated through and blended, stirring frequently. Pour over the chicken. Combine the crackers and poppy seeds in a bowl. Stir in the butter. Spread over the soup mixture. Bake at 350 degrees for 30 to 40 minutes.

Serves 6 to 8

Southern Fried Chicken

1 chicken, skin removed and
chicken cut up
Salt and pepper to taste
2 cups buttermilk
2 cups all-purpose flour
1 cup safflower oil

Soak the chicken in salted water to cover for 1 to 2 hours, if desired. Drain and pat dry, discarding the liquid. Season the chicken with salt and pepper. Dip in the buttermilk and roll in the flour, coating well. Heat the oil in a large heavy skillet until very hot. Fry the chicken in batches in the hot oil for 20 to 30 minutes, turning once. Cubed steak or pork chops may be substituted for the chicken; cook for 10 to 12 minutes, turning once.

Serves 6 to 8

Fried Okra

1 egg
Salt and pepper to taste
1 pound okra, sliced into 1/2-inch pieces
1 to 2 tablespoons all-purpose flour
1 cup cornmeal
2 to 3 cups canola oil

Combine the egg with a pinch of salt in a medium bowl. Season with pepper and beat lightly with a fork. Add the okra and toss to coat. Place the flour in a shallow dish. Mix the cornmeal, salt and pepper in a shallow dish. Coat the okra first with the flour, and then with the cornmeal mixture. Heat 1 to 2 inches of canola oil in a large heavy skillet over high heat until amost smoking. Fry the okra in the hot oil until brown and crisp. Drain on paper towels.

Serves 4 to 6

Southern-Style Creamed Corn

8 ears of corn
1 tablespoon all-purpose flour
2 tablespoons sugar
1/2 teaspoon pepper
Salt to taste
1 cup heavy cream
1/2 cup cold water
2 tablespoons bacon drippings
1 tablespoon butter

Cut the kernels from the corn into a bowl, using a sharp knife. Scrape the cobs with the back of the knife blade, releasing the milky liquid into the bowl. Combine the flour, sugar, pepper and salt in a bowl. Stir in the corn, cream and water. Heat the bacon drippings in a large heavy skillet over medium-high heat. Stir in the corn mixture and reduce the heat to medium. Cook until creamy and thick, stirring constantly. Stir in the butter just before serving.

Serves 4

Mashed Potatoes

12 ounces Idaho potatoes, peeled and cut into large pieces
3/4 teaspoon salt
1/2 to 1 cup heavy cream or milk
1/4 cup (1/2 stick) butter
1/2 teaspoon freshly ground white pepper

Combine the potatoes with enough water to cover by 1 inch in a large saucepan. Add the salt and bring to a boil. Boil for 12 minutes or just until fork-tender. Remove from the heat and drain, discarding the cooking liquid. Combine the potatoes, cream, butter and pepper in a mixing bowl. Beat at medium speed until smooth.

Serves 5

Sweet Potato Casserole

3 cups mashed cooked sweet potatoes
1 cup sugar
2 eggs, lightly beaten
1/3 cup orange juice
1/4 cup (1/2 stick) margarine, softened
1 teaspoon vanilla extract
1 cup packed brown sugar
1/3 cup all-purpose flour
1/3 cup margarine, melted
1 cup pecans, chopped

Mix the sweet potatoes, sugar, eggs, orange juice, 1/4 cup margarine and the vanilla in a bowl. Spoon into a greased baking dish. Mix the brown sugar, flour, 1/3 cup margarine and the pecans in a bowl. Crumble over the sweet potato mixture. Bake at 350 degrees for 25 to 30 minutes.

Serves 6

Strawberry Pretzel Salad

2 2/3 cups crushed pretzels
3/4 cup (1 1/2 sticks) butter, melted
3 tablespoons sugar
8 ounces cream cheese, softened
1 cup sugar
8 ounces whipped topping
1 (6-ounce) package strawberry gelatin
2 cups boiling water
16 ounces frozen sliced strawberries, thawed

Mix the pretzels, butter and 3 tablespoons sugar in a bowl. Spread in a 9×13-inch baking dish. Bake at 425 degrees for 10 minutes. Let stand until cool. Beat the cream cheese and 1 cup sugar in a mixing bowl until light and fluffy. Fold in the whipped topping. Spread over the pretzel layer. Dissolve the gelatin in the boiling water in a bowl. Stir in the strawberries. Chill for 15 minutes or until thickened. Stir and pour over the cream cheese layer. Chill, covered, for 3 to 10 hours or until set.

For a variation, use grape gelatin with blueberries or peach gelatin with sliced peaches. For a dessert version, substitute a fruit pie filling for the gelatin and fruit layer.

Serves 12 to 15

Mrs. Lena's Dressing

2 cups self-rising cornmeal
1 onion, finely chopped
2 ribs celery, chopped
2 eggs, lightly beaten
$1\frac{1}{2}$ cups buttermilk
$\frac{1}{4}$ cup vegetable oil
8 slices bread, lightly toasted and
  cut into cubes
2 or 3 (10-ounce) cans cream of chicken soup
4 eggs, lightly beaten
2 cups (or more) chicken broth
1 teaspoon poultry seasoning
1 teaspoon sage

Mix the cornmeal, onion, celery, 2 eggs, the buttermilk and oil in a bowl. Pour into a 9-inch baking pan or ovenproof skillet. Bake at 425 degrees for 20 to 25 minutes. Let stand until cool. Crumble into a large bowl. Add the bread, soup, 4 eggs, 2 cups broth, the poultry seasoning and sage and mix well. Pour into a 9×13-inch baking pan. Bake at 350 degrees for 60 to 75 minutes. Add additional broth around the edges as the dressing browns if needed to prevent it from drying out. You may add 2 to 3 cups shredded cooked chicken breast to the dressing before baking, if desired.

Serves 12

Deep South Corn Bread

$^{1}/_{3}$ cup corn oil
$1^{1}/_{2}$ cups self-rising cornmeal
2 tablespoons sugar
1 cup buttermilk
1 egg, lightly beaten

Heat the corn oil in a heavy cast-iron skillet in the oven at 450 degrees. Maintain the oven temperature. Mix the cornmeal, sugar, buttermilk and egg in a bowl. Pour into the hot skillet. Bake for 15 to 20 minutes or until brown.

Serves 6 to 8

Honeymoon Rolls

2 cups self-rising flour
1 cup (2 sticks) margarine, softened
1 cup sour cream
1 teaspoon salt

Mix the flour, margarine, sour cream and salt in a bowl. Shape the dough into balls or scoop into muffin cups. Bake at 400 degrees for 12 to 15 minutes.

Makes 2 dozen

Mrs. Rachel's Magnolia Café Biscuits with Chocolate Gravy

Biscuits
1/3 cup shortening
2 cups self-rising flour
2/3 cup buttermilk

Chocolate Gravy
2 cups sugar
6 tablespoons baking cocoa
2 cups milk
Salt to taste
1/4 cup all-purpose flour
1 cup water

For the biscuits, cut the shortening into the flour in a bowl until crumbly. Add the buttermilk gradually, mixing until a soft dough forms. Knead into a ball on a floured surface. Pat to 1/2 inch thick. Cut with a 2-inch biscuit cutter. Place on a baking sheet and bake at 450 degrees until golden brown.

For the gravy, mix the sugar, baking cocoa, milk and salt in a saucepan. Bring to a rolling boil, stirring frequently. Reduce the heat to medium. Remove from the heat and stir in a mixture of the flour and water. Serve with the biscuits.

Serves 12

Mrs. Rachel Smith has been baking these biscuits for the Madison Academy family for more than thirty years. The school's fall fund-raiser, Southern Tradition, wouldn't be the same without them.

Old-Fashioned Shortcakes

2 cups self-rising flour
1/3 cup sugar
2/3 cup shortening
2 tablespoons cold butter
1 egg
1/2 to 2/3 cup milk

Mix the flour and sugar in a bowl. Cut in the shortening and butter until crumbly. Beat the egg and milk lightly in a bowl. Stir into the flour mixture. The batter will be very thick and sticky. Drop by large scoopfuls onto a greased baking sheet. Spread into 4-inch circles. Bake on the top oven rack at 375 degrees until the edges are brown. For Strawberry Shortcakes, serve with sweetened whipped cream and sliced strawberries.

Makes 12

Lottie's Fried Apple Pies

4 cups dried apples
2 cups water
1/2 to 3/4 cup sugar, or to taste
Salt to taste
3 cups all-purpose flour
1 teaspoon salt
3/4 cup shortening
1 egg, beaten
1/4 cup water
1 teaspoon vinegar
1 tablespoon vegetable oil
Shortening

Combine the apples and 2 cups water in a saucepan and bring to a boil. Reduce the heat and simmer, covered, for 30 minutes or until tender. Mash slightly. Stir in the sugar and salt to taste; set aside.

Combine the flour and 1 teaspoon salt in a bowl. Cut in 3/4 cup shortening until crumbly. Mix the egg and 1/4 cup water in a bowl. Sprinkle over the flour mixture. Add the vinegar and stir lightly until the mixture forms a ball. Wrap in waxed paper and chill for 1 hour or until needed.

Divide the pastry into halves and roll each 1/4 to 1/3 inch thick on waxed paper. Cut with a 5-inch biscuit cutter. For each pie, spoon 2 tablespoons of the apple mixture onto one half of one round. Moisten the edge of the round with water and fold over the filling to form a half-moon. Crimp the edge using a fork dipped in flour.

Heat the oil and enough shortening to yield 1/2 inch of liquid to 375 degrees in a large heavy skillet. Fry the pies in the hot shortening until golden brown on both sides, turning once. Drain on a clean nonrecycled brown paper bag. Dried peaches or dried apricots may be substituted for the apples.

Makes 1 1/2 dozen

Julie's French Apple Pie

3 cups sliced apples
3/4 cup granulated sugar
1 teaspoon cinnamon
1 unbaked (9-inch) pie shell
Butter
1 cup self-rising flour
1/2 cup chopped pecans (optional)
1/2 cup packed brown sugar
1/2 cup (1 stick) butter, softened

Toss the apples with the granulated sugar and cinnamon in a bowl. Spoon into the pie shell and dot with butter. Mix the flour, pecans, brown sugar and 1/2 cup butter in a bowl until crumbly. Sprinkle over the apples. Bake at 400 degrees for 45 to 55 minutes.

Serves 8

Chess Pie

1/2 cup (1 stick) butter
1 1/2 cups sugar
3 eggs, beaten
1 tablespoon white vinegar
1 tablespoon vanilla extract
1 unbaked (9-inch) pie shell

Combine the butter and sugar in a saucepan. Cook until the butter is melted and the sugar is dissolved, stirring constantly. Remove from the heat. Add the eggs and beat until smooth. Stir in the vinegar and vanilla. Pour into the pie shell. Bake at 325 degrees for 40 minutes.

Serves 8

Southern Pecan Pie

1 cup sugar
1/2 cup corn syrup
1/4 cup (1/2 stick) butter, softened
1 teaspoon vanilla extract
3 eggs, beaten
1 cup pecan halves
Never-Fail Pie Pastry (below)

Mix the sugar, corn syrup, butter and vanilla in a bowl until smooth. Stir in the eggs and pecans. Fit the pastry into a pie plate. Pour the pecan mixture into the pastry-lined pie plate. Bake at 400 degrees for 10 minutes. Reduce the oven temperature to 350 degrees and bake for 30 to 35 minutes.

Serves 8

Never-Fail Pie Pastry

1 cup all-purpose flour
1 teaspoon salt
1/2 cup shortening
1/4 cup ice water

Mix the flour and salt in a bowl. Cut in the shortening until crumbly. Add the water gradually, mixing constantly by hand until the mixture forms a ball. Chill, wrapped in plastic wrap, for 30 minutes.

Makes 1 (1-crust) pie pastry

Grandma's Sunday Chocolate Pie

1 cup sugar
1/3 cup self-rising flour
3 tablespoons baking cocoa
3 cups milk
3 egg yolks
1 tablespoon butter
3 egg whites, at room temperature
1/2 teaspoon salt
3 to 4 tablespoons sugar
1 baked (9-inch) pie shell

Combine 1 cup sugar, the flour and baking cocoa in a saucepan. Stir in the milk and egg yolks. Cook over medium heat until thickened to the consistency of pudding, stirring constantly. Remove from the heat and set the saucepan in a larger bowl filled with ice water. Stir the butter into the chocolate mixture.

Beat the egg whites and salt in a chilled metal mixing bowl with chilled beaters until soft peaks form. Add 3 to 4 tablespoons sugar 1 tablespoon at a time, beating constantly until stiff peaks form. Stir the chocolate mixture and pour into the pie shell. Top with the meringue, sealing to the edge. Bake at 450 degrees until the meringue is brown.

For Coconut Pie or Banana Pie, omit the baking cocoa and add 1 cup shredded coconut or 1 cup sliced banana after the filling has thickened. Sprinkle additional coconut over the meringue before baking if making the Coconut Pie.

Serves 6

MEME'S CREAM CHEESE POUND CAKE

3 cups sifted cake flour
1/2 teaspoon salt
1 cup (2 sticks) margarine, softened
1/2 cup (1 stick) butter, softened
8 ounces cream cheese, softened
3 cups sugar
6 eggs
1 1/2 teaspoons vanilla extract

Mix the flour and salt together. Cream the margarine, butter, cream cheese and sugar in a mixing bowl until light and fluffy. Add the eggs one at a time, mixing well after each addition. Add the flour mixture and mix well. Stir in the vanilla. Pour into a buttered and floured tube pan. Bake at 325 degrees for 1 hour and 20 minutes.

Serves 12 to 15

DENNISON FARM STRAWBERRY CAKE

1 (2-layer) package white cake mix
1 (3-ounce) package strawberry gelatin
3 tablespoons all-purpose flour
1 cup vegetable oil
1/2 cup milk
4 eggs
1 (16-ounce) package frozen sliced strawberries
8 ounces cream cheese, softened
1 (1-pound) package confectioners' sugar

Mix the cake mix, gelatin, flour, oil and milk in a mixing bowl. Add the eggs one at a time, mixing well after each addition. Fold in three-fourths of the strawberries. Pour into three greased and floured 9-inch cake pans. Bake at 325 degrees for 30 minutes. Cool in the pans for 10 minutes. Remove to a wire rack to cool completely. Drain the remaining strawberres. Beat the cream cheese, confectioners' sugar and 3 tablespoons of the remaining strawberries in a mixing bowl until light and fluffy. Add any remaining strawberries, if desired. Spread between the layers and over the top and side of the cooled cake.

Serves 12

Big Mama's "Motor Coach" Red Velvet Cake

2 1/2 cups all-purpose flour
1 tablespoon baking cocoa
1/2 teaspoon salt
1 teaspoon baking soda
1 cup buttermilk
1 1/2 cups granulated sugar
1 1/4 cups vegetable oil
2 bottles red food coloring
2 eggs, lightly beaten
1/2 cup (1 stick) butter, softened
8 ounces cream cheese, softened
1 (1-pound) package confectioners' sugar
1 teaspoon vanilla extract
1 cup chopped pecans

Sift the flour, baking cocoa and salt together. Dissolve the baking soda in the buttermilk in a bowl. Cream the granulated sugar, oil and food coloring in a mixing bowl. Add the flour mixture, buttermilk and eggs alternately to the creamed mixture, mixing well after each addition. Pour into two greased and floured 9-inch cake pans. Bake at 350 degrees for 30 to 40 minutes. Cool in the pans for 10 minutes. Remove to a wire rack to cool completely.

Cream the butter, cream cheese and confectioners' sugar in a mixing bowl until light and fluffy. Stir in the vanilla and pecans. Spread between the layers and over the top and side of the cooled cake.

Serves 12

SARGE AT LARGE: *One of Sarge's jobs is directing bus tours at home and all over the country. Some of you have seen her traveling, clad in her famous red blazer, with a weary group of travelers hustling to keep up with her. Her favorite mode of transportation is a Knoxville Tours* "Motor Coach." *But woe is the pilgrim who calls it a lowly bus!*

One, Two, Three, Four Cake

3 cups all-purpose flour
1/2 teaspoon baking soda
Pinch of salt
1 cup (2 sticks) butter, softened
2 cups sugar
4 eggs
1 cup buttermilk
1 teaspoon vanilla extract
Mother's Chocolate Frosting (below)

Sift the flour, baking soda and salt together. Cream the butter and sugar in a mixing bowl for 10 minutes or until light and fluffy. Add the eggs one at a time, mixing well after each addition. Add the dry ingredients and buttermilk alternately to the creamed mixture, mixing well after each addition. Stir in the vanilla. Pour into three greased and floured 8-inch cake pans. Bake at 350 degrees for 35 minutes. Cool in the pans for 10 minutes. Remove to a wire rack to cool completely. Spread the frosting between the layers and over the top and side of the cooled cake. This cake may be prepared in a greased and floured tube pan and baked for 1 hour.

Serves 12 to 15

Mother's Chocolate Frosting

2 cups sugar
1/2 cup baking cocoa
6 tablespoons margarine
1/3 cup milk
Pinch of salt
1 teaspoon vanilla extract

Combine the sugar, baking cocoa, margarine, milk and salt in a saucepan. Bring to a boil, stirring constantly. Boil for 1 minute. Remove from the heat and stir in the vanilla. Pour into a heatproof bowl and beat until of a spreading consistency.

Makes about 2 cups

Chocolate Buttermilk Cake

Cake

1 cup all-purpose flour
2 cups sugar
1 cup (2 sticks) butter
1/4 cup baking cocoa
1 cup water
1/2 cup buttermilk
2 eggs, lightly beaten
1 teaspoon baking soda
1 teaspoon vanilla extract

Chocolate Pecan Frosting

1/2 cup (1 stick) butter
6 tablespoons milk
1/4 cup baking cocoa
1 (1-pound) package confectioners' sugar
1 teaspoon vanilla extract
1 cup chopped pecans, toasted (optional)

For the cake, combine the flour and sugar in a mixing bowl. Combine the butter, baking cocoa and water in a saucepan. Bring to a boil gradually, stirring frequently. Add to the flour mixture and mix well. Combine the buttermilk, eggs, baking soda and vanilla in a bowl. Add to the flour mixture and mix well. Pour into a greased and floured 9×13-inch baking pan. Bake at 325 degrees for 45 minutes.

For the frosting, combine the butter, milk and baking cocoa in a saucepan. Bring to a boil, stirring frequently. Remove from the heat and stir in the confectioners' sugar, vanilla and pecans. Spread over the hot cake.

Serves 8 to 10

When making a chocolate cake or chocolate brownies, use baking cocoa to dust the pan. You will not have the white film that is sometimes left after flouring a pan with white flour.

"Oh, Oh...Oatmeal" Cookies

1/2 cup shortening
1/2 cup (1 stick) butter, softened
1 cup granulated sugar
1/2 cup packed brown sugar
1 egg, beaten
1 teaspoon vanilla extract
1 1/2 cups all-purpose flour
1 teaspoon baking soda
1 teaspoon salt
1 teaspoon cinnamon (optional)
1 1/2 cups rolled oats
3/4 cup chopped pecans

Cream the shortening, butter, granulated sugar and brown sugar in a mixing bowl until light and fluffy. Add the egg, vanilla, flour, baking soda, salt, cinnamon and oats in the order listed, mixing well after each addition. Stir in the pecans. Chill, covered, for 1 hour. Shape the dough into walnut-size balls and place 2 inches apart on an ungreased cookie sheet. Flatten with a buttered glass dipped in additional granulated sugar. Bake at 350 degrees for 10 to 12 minutes.

Makes 4 to 5 dozen

Thimble Cookies

2 cups all-purpose flour
1/2 teaspoon salt
1/2 cup (1 stick) butter, softened
1/2 cup shortening
1/2 cup packed brown sugar
2 egg yolks
2 teaspoons vanilla extract
2 egg whites, beaten
1 1/2 cups pecans, finely chopped
2 cups confectioners' sugar
1/4 cup whipping cream

Sift the flour and salt together. Beat the butter and shortening in a mixing bowl until smooth. Add the brown sugar and beat until light and fluffy. Add the egg yolks and vanilla and mix well. Add the sifted dry ingredients and mix well. Shape into balls. Dip in the egg whites and roll in the pecans. Arrange 1 inch apart on a greased cookie sheet. Bake at 375 degrees for 5 minutes. Remove from the oven and make an indentation in the center of each cookie immediately with a buttered thimble. Bake for 6 to 8 minutes longer. Beat the confectioners' sugar and cream in a bowl. Fill the indentations in the cookies with the icing. Food coloring may be added to the icing, if desired.

Makes 2 to 3 dozen

Grains of Knowledge

Huntsville Female Seminary was one of the first girls' schools in Alabama. The seminary was located on the south side of Randolph Street, east of Lincoln Street. It replaced the Huntsville Female Academy organized in 1830. The new teaching staff were protégés of Catharine Beecher of the Hartford Female Seminary in Connecticut. The school offered a more highly structured and advanced curriculum than most southern female colleges. In 1854, George Steele designed a new Gothic façade for the building. The seminary closed in 1862, but the building was used as a hospital for smallpox victims during the Civil War. The seminary reopened in 1867 and was used for a variety of educational institutions through 1910. It was demolished in 1912 by A. M. Booth. Some of the building's original architectural elements were harvested and used in the present structure found on the site today. The school is shown here with students in 1888.

Grains of Knowledge

Breakfast and Breads

"Ex-tree" Good Eggs Monterey

12 eggs
1/2 cup all-purpose flour
2 (4-ounce) cans diced green chiles, drained
4 cups (16 ounces) shredded Monterey Jack cheese
2 cups small curd cottage cheese
1/2 cup (1 stick) butter, melted
1 teaspoon baking powder
1/2 teaspoon salt

Beat the eggs and flour in a mixing bowl until combined. Stir in the green chiles, Monterey Jack cheese, cottage cheese, butter, baking powder and salt. Pour into a greased 9×13-inch baking dish. Bake at 350 degrees for 35 minutes or until the top is golden brown and the center is firm. Garnish with salsa and sour cream.

Serves 10 to 12

Sarge at Large: *Sarge's pronunciation of this dish just makes you want more!*

French Morning Eggs

1/2 cup (1 stick) butter
6 tablespoons all-purpose flour
2 3/4 cups milk
2 teaspoons salt
1/2 teaspoon white pepper
1/4 teaspoon red pepper
12 hard-cooked eggs, sliced
1 1/2 cups crushed butter crackers

Melt the butter in the top of a double boiler set over boiling water. Stir in the flour. Add the milk gradually, stirring constantly. Stir in the salt, white pepper and red pepper. Cook until thickened, stirring constantly. Layer the eggs, sauce and crackers one-half at a time in a 9×13-inch baking dish. Bake at 300 degrees until bubbly and light brown. This dish may be assembled 1 day in advance. Cover and chill. Let stand at room temperature for 1 hour before baking.

Serves 10

Pesto Strata

1 (1 1/4-pound) loaf sourdough bread
8 ounces cream cheese, cut into cubes
8 ounces mozzarella cheese, shredded
1 cup pesto
6 ounces thinly sliced prosciutto
1 pound tomatoes, thinly sliced
6 eggs
1 1/2 cups fat-free half-and-half
1 1/2 teaspoons salt
Pepper to taste
2 cups (8 ounces) shredded Cheddar cheese

Cut the bread into 1/2-inch slices. Layer the bread, cream cheese, mozzarella cheese, dollops of pesto, the prosciutto and tomatoes one-half at a time in a 9×13-inch baking dish sprayed with nonstick cooking spray. Cut or tear the bread as needed to fit snuggly in a single layer.

Whisk the eggs, half-and-half and salt in a bowl until combined. Season with pepper. Pour over the layers. Top with the Cheddar cheese. Chill, covered, for 2 to 10 hours. Let stand at room temperature for 20 minutes before baking. Bake at 350 degrees for 1 hour or until the strata is puffed, golden brown and lightly set in the center. Let stand for 10 minutes before slicing.

Serves 6 to 8

Breakfast Crescent Casserole

1 pound bulk pork sausage
3 eggs, beaten
2 (8-count) cans refrigerator crescent rolls
2 cups (8 ounces) shredded sharp
  Cheddar cheese

Brown the sausage in a skillet, stirring until crumbly. Drain on paper towels. Mix the eggs and sausage in a bowl. Fit one can of the crescent rolls over the bottom of a greased 9×11-inch baking dish, pressing the perforations to seal. Spread the sausage mixture over the crescent roll layer. Sprinkle with the cheese. Top with the remaining can of crescent rolls fitted to form a crust. Bake at 375 degrees for 20 to 30 minutes. Cut into squares.

Serve 8

Milla's Cheese Grits

1/2 cup (1 stick) butter, chopped
1 cup hot cooked grits
1 cup (4 ounces) shredded Cheddar cheese
1 tablespoon seasoned salt
1 teaspoon Worcestershire sauce
1 teaspoon Tabasco sauce
1 teaspoon paprika
2 eggs, beaten

Stir the butter into the hot grits in a bowl. Stir in the cheese, seasoned salt, Worcestershire sauce, Tabasco sauce and paprika. Let stand until cool. Add the eggs and mix well. Pour into a 2-quart baking dish. Bake at 350 degrees for 30 minutes or until the top is brown.

Serves 6 to 8

French Toast Soufflé

10 cups cubed white bread (about 16 slices)
8 ounces 1/3 less-fat cream cheese, softened
8 eggs
1 1/2 cups 2% milk
2/3 cup half-and-half
1/2 cup maple syrup
1/2 teaspoon vanilla extract
2 tablespoons confectioners' sugar
3/4 cup maple syrup

Arrange the bread in a 9×13-inch baking dish sprayed with nonstick cooking spray. Beat the cream cheese in a mixing bowl at medium speed until smooth. Add the eggs one at a time, mixing well after each addition. Add the milk, half-and-half, 1/2 cup maple syrup and the vanilla. Beat until smooth. Pour over the bread. Chill, covered, for 8 to 10 hours. Let stand at room temperature for 30 minutes before baking.

Bake at 375 degrees for 50 minutes or until the center is firm. Dust with the confectioners' sugar. Serve 3/4 cup maple syrup on the side.

Serves 12

Club Waffles

2 cups baking mix
3 tablespoons vegetable oil
1 egg, beaten
1 1/3 cups club soda

Mix the baking mix, oil and egg in a bowl. Stir in the club soda. Bake in a very hot Belgian waffle iron sprayed with nonstick cooking spray until the waffles are golden brown.

Serves 6 to 8

Snow White Waffles

3 1/2 cups self-rising flour
1 cup sugar
2 teaspoons baking powder
1 teaspoon salt
2 eggs, beaten
4 cups milk
2 cups heavy cream
1/4 cup water
1 cup (2 sticks) butter, melted
1/2 cup butter-flavor shortening
2 teaspoons vanilla extract
Confectioners' sugar
Maple syrup

Mix the flour, sugar, baking powder and salt together. Mix the eggs, milk, cream and water in a bowl. Add the dry ingredients gradually, stirring constantly until combined. Stir in the butter, shortening and vanilla. Chill, covered, for 8 to 10 hours. Bake in a waffle iron until brown, using the manufacturer's directions. Dust with confectioners' sugar and serve maple syrup on the side.

Makes 20

Sea Island Scones

3 1/4 cups all-purpose flour
1/3 cup sugar
2 1/4 tablespoons baking powder
2 eggs
1 2/3 cups butter, softened
1/2 cup whipping cream
1/3 cup milk
1/3 cup currants, raisins, blueberries or
  chopped dried apricots
Freshly whipped cream or butter

Sift the flour, sugar and baking powder together. Beat the eggs, butter, cream and milk at low speed in a mixing bowl until combined. Add the sifted dry ingredients and mix well. Roll or pat to 3/4 inch thick on a lightly floured surface and cut with a 2 1/4-inch biscuit cutter. Arrange on a baking sheet. Bake at 350 degrees for 22 minutes. Serve topped with whipped cream or butter.

Makes 2 dozen

Spiced Golden Raisin Bran Muffins

1 (18-ounce) package bran cereal
3 cups boiling water
2 1/2 cups all-purpose flour
2 1/2 cups whole wheat flour
2 cups granulated sugar
1 cup packed brown sugar
5 teaspoons baking soda
1 tablespoon salt
2 teaspoons cinnamon
1 teaspoon nutmeg
1/2 teaspoon ground cloves
Dash of ginger
4 cups buttermilk
4 eggs, beaten
1 1/4 cups vegetable oil
1 tablespoon vanilla extract
1 to 2 cups golden raisins
1 cup chopped pecans

Soak the cereal in the water in a bowl; set aside. Mix the all-purpose flour, whole wheat flour, granulated sugar, brown sugar, baking soda, salt, cinnamon, nutmeg, cloves and ginger in a large bowl. Add the buttermilk, eggs, oil and vanilla. Stir until smooth. Stir in the cereal mixture, raisins and pecans. Fill greased muffin cups two-thirds full. Bake at 350 degrees for 12 to 15 minutes.

For a variation, substitute 1 1/2 cups shredded carrots for the golden raisins.

Makes 6 dozen

Pecan Pie Muffins

1 cup packed light brown sugar
1/2 cup all-purpose flour
1/2 cup chopped pecans, toasted
2 eggs, beaten
2/3 cup butter, softened

Mix the brown sugar, flour and pecans in a bowl. Beat the eggs and butter in a mixing bowl until smooth. Add the brown sugar mixture and beat just until combined. Fill paper-lined muffin cups two-thirds full. Bake at 350 degrees for 20 to 25 minutes. Remove to a wire rack to cool completely.

Makes 6

Best-Ever Banana Bread

Bread
1 cup granulated sugar
1/2 cup (1 stick) butter, softened
1/2 cup sour cream
2 eggs, lightly beaten
1 teaspoon vanilla extract
1 cup mashed overripe bananas
1 1/2 cups all-purpose flour
1 teaspoon baking soda
1/2 teaspoon salt
1/2 cup chopped pecans
1 tablespoon turbinado sugar

Brown Sugar Glaze (optional)
5 tablespoons brown sugar
2 tablespoons cream or milk
3 tablespoons butter

For the bread, beat the granulated sugar, butter, sour cream, eggs and vanilla in a mixing bowl until smooth. Stir in the bananas. Mix the flour, baking soda and salt together. Add to the banana mixture and beat for 1 minute. Fold in the pecans. Pour into a greased and floured 5×9-inch loaf pan. Sprinkle with the turbinado sugar. Bake at 350 degrees for 1 hour or until a wooden pick inserted in the center comes out clean. Remove to a wire rack to cool.

For the glaze, combine the brown sugar, cream, and butter in a saucepan. Bring to a boil. Pour over the bread while on the wire rack.

Serve 6 to 8

When ripe or overripe bananas are not available for making banana bread, use grated green bananas. The consistency and flavor are similar to mashed overripe bananas.

Tropical Coffee Cake

1 1/2 cups all-purpose flour, sifted
1 cup sugar
2 teaspoons baking powder
1/2 teaspoon salt
1 cup pineapple yogurt
1/2 cup vegetable oil
2 eggs, lightly beaten
1 cup sweetened flaked coconut
1/3 cup sugar
1 teaspoon cinnamon

Mix the flour, 1 cup sugar, the baking powder, salt, yogurt, oil and eggs in a bowl. Stir seventy to eighty strokes with a wooden spoon or until blended. Pour into a greased 9×9-inch baking pan. Mix the coconut, 1/3 cup sugar and the cinnamon in a small bowl. Sprinkle over the batter. Bake at 350 degrees for 35 minutes.

Serves 8 to 12

Mexican Corn Bread

1 cup self-rising cornmeal
1/3 cup vegetable oil
2/3 cup milk
2 eggs, lightly beaten
1 (5-ounce) can cream-style corn
1 (4-ounce) can diced green chiles,
  or 1 (4-ounce) can chopped jalapeño chiles
1 cup (4 ounces) shredded Cheddar cheese

Mix the cornmeal, oil, milk, eggs, corn, green chiles and cheese in a bowl in the order listed, mixing well after each addition. Pour into a greased 9×9-inch baking pan. Bake at 400 degrees for 45 minutes.

Serves 8 to 10

Italian "Gon-dough-lah" Bread

1/4 cup (1/2 stick) butter, melted
1 teaspoon poppy seeds
1/2 teaspoon dried parsley flakes
1 teaspoon dried onion flakes
1/2 teaspoon garlic salt
1/2 teaspoon seasoned salt
1/2 teaspoon Italian seasoning
2 (10-count) cans flaky refrigerator biscuits
1/4 cup (1/2 stick) butter, melted

Pour 1/4 cup butter into a bundt pan. Sprinkle with the poppy seeds, parsley, onion flakes, garlic salt, seasoned salt and Italian seasoning. Arrange the biscuits on their sides around the pan. Pour 1/4 cup melted butter over the biscuits. Bake at 400 degrees for 15 minutes.

For Honey Cinnamon Bread, use honey butter biscuits and substitute raisins and cinnamon-sugar for the seasonings.

Serves 12

SARGE AT LARGE: *Being proud of her town comes easily for Sarge. When the new Bridge Street Town Center opened, she was so excited about the beautiful lake and the "Gon-dough-lah" (gondola) rides!*

Sweet Cream Biscuits

4 cups all-purpose flour
1 teaspoon salt
2 tablespoons baking powder
$1^1/_2$ cups heavy cream
$^1/_4$ cup (about) water

Sift the flour, salt and baking powder into a large bowl. Add the cream gradually, stirring constantly with a fork just until the dry ingredients are moistened. Add the water gradually, stirring constantly until crumbly. Knead ten times on a lightly floured surface. Roll $^3/_4$ inch thick. Cut with a small floured biscuit cutter and arrange on a baking sheet. Bake at 450 degrees for 12 minutes or until golden brown. Serve immediately.

Makes 3 dozen

Princess Rolls

2 cups self-rising flour
1 teaspoon sugar
1 teaspoon salt
$^1/_4$ cup mayonnaise
1 cup milk

Mix the flour, sugar and salt in a bowl. Stir in the mayonnaise and milk. Fill greased muffin cups three-fourths full. Bake at 450 degrees for 12 minutes. These may be prepared in miniature muffin cups; reduce the baking time.

Makes 1 dozen

Crescent Dinner Rolls

2 envelopes dry yeast
1 tablespoon sugar
1/4 cup warm water
4 cups (or more) all-purpose flour
1/2 cup sugar
1 teaspoon baking powder
1 teaspoon salt
3/4 cup shortening
1 3/4 cups buttermilk
1 teaspoon baking soda

Dissolve the yeast and 1 tablespoon sugar in the warm water; set aside. Sift the flour, 1/2 cup sugar, the baking powder and salt into a bowl. Cut in the shortening. Heat the buttermilk in a saucepan until slightly warm. Dissolve the baking soda in the warm buttermilk. Remove from the heat and stir in the yeast mixture. Stir into the flour mixture with a wooden spoon. Add additional flour if the dough is sticky. Knead on a lightly floured surface until the dough forms a ball. Chill, covered, for 1 to 2 days.

Roll out on a lightly floured surface and let stand for 1 hour. Divide the dough into five equal portions. Shape each portion into a ball. Roll each ball into a rectangle. Cut each rectangle into eight wedges and arrange on a greased baking sheet. Bake at 375 degrees for 15 minutes.

For Cinnamon Pecan Rolls, divide the dough into two portions. Roll 1/4 inch thick and brush with melted butter. Sprinkle with cinnamon, sugar, raisins and chopped toasted pecans. Bake for 30 to 35 minutes. Mix 1 cup confectioners' sugar, vanilla extract to taste and enough water to reach an icing consistency. Spread over the sweet rolls.

Makes 3 dozen

LIFTOFF

In the spring of 1950, a team of 118 German scientists under the direction of Wernher von Braun arrived in Huntsville to work for the Army rocket program. After arriving, the von Braun team developed the first surface-to-surface missile, which later became known as the Redstone Rocket.

Huntsville's Redstone Arsenal, birthplace of the free world's first earth satellite, broke all records for growth and progress during the early 1950s. Redstone Arsenal was and continues to be one of Huntsville's biggest assets, industries, and payroll sources. In 1958, the payroll topped $125 million, and this money was reflected in the prosperity of the entire area. This led to the founding of the National Aeronautics and Space Administration (NASA).

In 1960, Redstone Arsenal was named Marshall Space Flight Center and Dr. von Braun was named as its director. The NASA engineers were given the task of designing a large spacecraft that could carry a man to the moon. On July 16, 1969, with the aid of the Saturn V rocket, this mission was carried out.

LIFTOFF

STARTERS AND SIPS

Lasagna "Roll-a-den-dras"

1 (8-ounce) package lasagna noodles
16 ounces ricotta cheese
2 eggs, beaten
1 (10-ounce) package frozen chopped spinach, thawed and drained
2 cups (8 ounces) shredded mozzarella cheese
1 teaspoon marjoram
1 teaspoon basil
1 (26- to 32-ounce) jar spaghetti sauce
6 to 8 ounces Parmesan cheese, grated

Cook the pasta according to the package directions; drain. Lay the pasta on waxed paper sprayed lightly with nonstick cooking spray. Mix the ricotta cheese, eggs, spinach, mozzarella cheese, marjoram and basil in a bowl. Spread evenly over the pasta. Cut the pasta into halves. Roll the pasta and cut into halves again. Spread three-fourths of the spaghetti sauce in an 11×13-inch baking dish. Arrange the pasta rolls curly side up with sides touching in the baking dish. Top with the remaining sauce and sprinkle with the Parmesan cheese. Bake, covered with foil, at 350 degrees for 35 to 40 minutes. These rolls may be frozen before baking.

Serves 15

Sarge at Large: *On a trip to the Biltmore Estates, Sarge was exuberant with information pertaining to the foliage on the grounds. "As you can see, the* roll-a-den-dra *(rhododendron) and mountain Laura (laurel) are in full bloom." After we regained our composure, she asked (as is her custom), "What did I say?" She laughed right along with us. What a trouper!*

Reuben Egg Roll Wraps

1 1/2 cups sauerkraut, drained
1 tablespoon sesame seeds
Juice of 1/2 lemon
1 egg
1 tablespoon water
8 egg roll wrappers
4 ounces thinly sliced Swiss cheese, cut into strips
6 ounces thinly sliced corned beef, cut into strips
2 tablespoons prepared mustard
1 cup vegetable oil
1 bottle Thousand Island salad dressing

Sauté the sauerkraut and sesame seeds in a skillet over medium-high heat until most of the moisture has evaporated and the sauerkraut begins to brown. Stir in the lemon juice. Whisk the egg and water in a bowl until combined.

Place an egg roll wrapper on the diagonal on a flat surface. Brush the edges with the egg wash. Place one piece of cheese about 1 inch above the bottom corner. Layer with corned beef strips and about 3 tablespoons of the sauerkraut mixture. Drizzle with the mustard. Fold the bottom corner up over the filling. Fold in both sides over the filling. Roll from the bottom toward the top corner. Repeat with the remaining egg roll wrappers and fillings.

Heat the oil to 360 degrees in a large skillet over medium-high heat. Fry the egg rolls in two batches for 5 to 7 minutes each or until crisp and brown, turning frequently. Drain on paper towels. Serve with the salad dressing on the side for dipping.

Makes 8

Parmesan Baguette Bites

8 ounces cream cheese, softened
1/2 cup mayonnaise
1/4 cup (1 ounce) grated Parmesan cheese
1 tablespoon chopped chives
3/4 teaspoon grated onion
1/4 teaspoon red pepper
1 French baguette

Mix the cream cheese, mayonnaise, Parmesan cheese, chives, onion and red pepper in a bowl. Slice the baguette into halves horizontally. Spread the cheese mixture on both halves and place on a baking sheet. Bake at 350 degrees for 15 minutes. Cut into bite-size pieces.

Serves 30

Store large pieces of Parmesan cheese or Romano cheese in an airtight container with two or three sugar cubes. The sugar will absorb the moisture and keep the cheese from becoming moldy. Replace the sugar cubes once they become soggy.

Chicken and Black Bean Salsa Roll-Ups

2 (12-ounce) cans all-white-meat chicken, drained
1 (15-ounce) can black beans, rinsed and drained
1 (16-ounce) jar chunky salsa
16 ounces cream cheese, softened
1 (12-count) package 10-inch wheat tortillas

Cook the chicken, beans and salsa in a skillet until heated through, stirring frequently. Remove from the heat and let stand for 10 minutes. Stir in the cream cheese. Chill, covered, for 2 to 10 hours or until thickened. Spoon 1/2 cup of the mixture onto one half of each tortilla. Roll tightly from the side with the mixture, allowing the pressure to spread the mixture evenly in the tortilla. Cut into 1/2-inch slices. Chill, covered, until serving time. Garnish with shredded Cheddar cheese and sour cream.

Serves 15 to 20

Cocktail Puffs with Chicken Pecan Filling

1/2 cup (1 stick) butter
1 cup water
1 cup sifted all-purpose flour
1/4 teaspoon salt
4 eggs
1/2 cup finely chopped pecans
2 tablespoons butter
1 1/2 cups finely chopped cooked chicken
1/2 cup mayonnaise
3 ounces cream cheese, softened

Melt 1/2 cup butter in a saucepan. Stir in the water, flour and salt. Cook until the mixture forms a ball, stirring constantly. Remove from the heat and add the eggs one at a time, mixing well after each addition. Drop by teaspoonfuls or pipe onto a greased baking sheet. Bake at 425 degrees for 20 minutes. Cool on a wire rack.

Combine the pecans and 2 tablespoons butter in a skillet. Cook until the pecans are brown, stirring frequently. Stir in the chicken, mayonnaise and cream cheese. Slice the top from each pastry. Spoon or pipe the chicken mixture into the pastries and replace the tops.

These may be frozen for up to 1 month in an airtight container. Bake, unthawed, at 350 degrees for 10 to 15 minutes.

Makes 6 dozen

Spinach Puffs

2 (10-ounce) packages frozen spinach
6 eggs, lightly beaten
2 cups chicken-flavor stuffing mix
1 cup (4 ounces) grated Parmesan cheese
3/4 cup (1 1/2 sticks) butter, softened
1/2 teaspoon salt
1/2 teaspoon freshly grated pepper, or to taste

Cook the spinach according to the package directions; drain. Mix the spinach, eggs, stuffing mix, cheese, butter, salt and pepper in a bowl. Shape into balls and place on a baking sheet. Freeze until firm. Remove to a sealable plastic freezer bag and freeze until baking time. Bake, unthawed, at 350 degrees for 15 to 20 minutes.

Serves 10 to 12

Hot Cheese Puffs

1 loaf unsliced white bread
2 egg whites
3 ounces cream cheese
4 ounces sharp Cheddar cheese, shredded
1/2 cup (1 stick) butter

Trim the crust from the bread and cut the bread into 1-inch cubes. Beat the egg whites in a mixing bowl until stiff peaks form. Combine the cream cheese, Cheddar cheese and butter in the top of a double boiler. Cook over simmering water until melted. Stir vigorously until combined. Remove from the heat and fold in the egg whites. Using a fork or skewer, dip the bread into the cheese mixture, coating well. Shake gently to remove any excess and place on a waxed paper-lined baking sheet. Chill, covered, for 8 to 10 hours. Bake at 400 degrees for 10 to 12 minutes or until golden brown.

These puffs may be frozen before baking. Let stand at room temperature for 30 minutes before baking.

Serves 40

Hidden Olives

8 ounces Cheddar cheese, shredded and softened
1/2 cup (1 stick) butter, softened
1/2 teaspoon sugar
1/2 teaspoon salt
1/4 teaspoon red pepper
1 cup all-purpose flour
54 pimento-stuffed olives

Mix the cheese and butter in a bowl. Stir in the sugar, salt and red pepper. Add the flour and mix well. Divide the dough into two equal portions. Divide each portion into twenty-seven equal pieces. Wrap each olive with a piece of the dough, sealing the olive inside. Arrange on a baking sheet. Bake at 350 degrees for 15 minutes.

Makes about 4 1/2 dozen

Bacon Marmalade Rounds

16 ounces sharp Cheddar cheese, shredded
8 ounces cream cheese, softened
3 egg yolks, lightly beaten
1/2 cup orange marmalade
40 melba toast rounds
8 ounces sliced bacon, crisp-cooked and crumbled

Mix the Cheddar cheese, cream cheese and egg yolks in a bowl. Add the marmalade and mix well. Spread over the melba toast rounds and arrange on a baking sheet. Sprinkle with the bacon. Broil until bubbly and heated through.

Makes 40

Dilled Salmon on Toasted Grain Bread

8 slices whole grain bread
1/4 cup mayonnaise
1/4 cup honey mustard
8 ounces smoked salmon, chopped
1/4 cup finely chopped red onion
1/4 cup chopped dill weed
2 tablespoons minced shallots
2 tablespoons drained capers, chopped
1 tablespoon lime juice
2 teaspoons olive oil
3/4 teaspoon kosher salt
1/2 teaspoon pepper

Trim the crusts from the bread. Toast the bread. Cut each slice into four strips; set aside. Mix the mayonnaise and mustard in a bowl; set aside. Mix the salmon, onion, dill weed, shallots, capers, lime juice, olive oil, salt and pepper in a bowl. Chill, covered, until serving time. To assemble, spread the mayonnaise mixture over the bread. Top each with some of the salmon mixture.

Makes 32

Country Club Baked Crab Meat Spread

32 ounces cream cheese, softened
2/3 cup mayonnaise
3 tablespoons confectioners' sugar
2 teaspoons onion juice
1 teaspoon prepared mustard
1 teaspoon granulated garlic
12 ounces lump crab meat

Mix the cream cheese, mayonnaise, confectioners' sugar, onion juice, mustard and garlic in a bowl. Fold in the crab meat. Pour into a greased 9×12-inch baking dish or two 1 1/2-quart chafing dish inserts. Bake at 325 degrees for 20 to 25 minutes or until bubbly. Serve with toast points or crackers.

Serves 36

Buffalo Chicken Dip

2 (12-ounce) cans all-white-meat chicken, drained
16 ounces cream cheese, softened
1 cup ranch salad dressing
1/2 cup Frank's Red Hot pepper sauce
8 ounces Velveeta cheese, crumbled, or 8 ounces Cheddar cheese, shredded

Mix the chicken, cream cheese, salad dressing and hot sauce in a bowl. Pour into a 9×13-inch glass baking dish. Sprinkle the Velveeta cheese over the top. Bake at 350 degrees until bubbly and heated through. Serve with corn chips or tortilla chips.

Serves 20

Mama Mia Pizzeria Dip

1 cup sour cream
8 ounces cream cheese, softened
1/4 cup (1 ounce) grated Parmesan cheese
1/2 cup pizza sauce
1 cup (4 ounces) shredded mozzarella cheese
1/2 cup chopped pepperoni

Mix the sour cream, cream cheese and Parmesan cheese in a bowl. Layer the sour cream mixture, pizza sauce, mozzarella cheese and pepperoni in a 10-inch baking dish. Bake at 350 degrees for 25 minutes or until the cheese is melted and bubbly. Serve warm with tortilla chips, pita chips or crackers.

Serves 10 to 15

Toasted Pecan Dip

$1/2$ cup chopped pecans
1 teaspoon butter
8 ounces cream cheese, softened
$1/2$ cup sour cream
2 teaspoons milk
3 ounces dried beef, finely chopped
1 small onion, finely chopped
$1/4$ cup finely chopped red bell pepper

Sauté the pecans in the butter in a saucepan until brown. Beat the cream cheese, sour cream and milk in a mixing bowl until smooth. Stir in the pecans, dried beef, onion and bell pepper. Spoon into a $1\,1/2$-quart baking dish. Bake at 350 degrees for 20 minutes. Serve with crackers.

For a variation, fill miniature pastry cups with the dip and bake according to the package directions.

Serves 20

Baked Cheese Trio

1 ($1\,1/2$-pound) round loaf sourdough bread
2 cups (8 ounces) shredded sharp Cheddar cheese
2 cups (8 ounces) shredded Monterey Jack cheese
$1\,1/2$ cups sour cream
8 ounces cream cheese, softened
1 (4-ounce) jar dried beef, chopped
1 (4-ounce) can diced green chiles
1 (2-ounce) jar pimento, drained
1 bunch green onions, chopped
1 tablespoon Worcestershire sauce

Cut the top from the bread and hollow out to make a shell. Cut the bread into cubes. Toast the cubed bread on a baking sheet at 350 degrees for 15 minutes. Mix the Cheddar cheese, Monterey Jack cheese, sour cream, cream cheese, dried beef, green chiles, pimento, green onions and Worcestershire sauce in a bowl. Spoon into the bread shell and replace the top. Wrap with foil and place on a baking sheet. Bake at 325 degrees for $1\,1/2$ hours. Serve warm with the toasted bread cubes, chips or crackers.

Serves 12 to 16

Bagalli Baked Brie and Artichoke Dip

1 small onion, chopped
1 teaspoon minced garlic
1 tablespoon olive oil
8 ounces cream cheese, chopped
1 cup heavy cream
1 (14-ounce) can artichoke hearts,
drained and chopped
2 or 3 green onions, chopped
1 tablespoon Worcestershire sauce
1 teaspoon salt
1 teaspoon pepper
1 (7-ounce) wedge Brie cheese

Sauté the onion and garlic in the olive oil in a skillet until the onion is translucent. Add the cream cheese and cream. Cook over low heat until the cream cheese is melted and the mixture is blended; do not boil. Stir in the artichokes, green onions, Worcestershire sauce, salt and pepper. Pour into a greased $1^{1}/_{2}$-quart baking dish. Remove and discard the rind from the Brie cheese. Cut the Brie cheese into cubes and press into the top of the dip. Bake at 350 degrees for 30 minutes or until bubbly.

Serves 20

Raspberry Praline Brie

1 (15-ounce) wheel Brie cheese
$^{3}/_{4}$ cup seedless raspberry jam
2 tablespoons brown sugar
1 teaspoon grated orange zest
$^{1}/_{2}$ cup chopped pecans

Place the cheese in the center of a greased glass pie plate. Mix the jam, brown sugar and orange zest in a bowl. Spread over the top of the cheese. Sprinkle with the pecans. Bake at 350 degrees for 15 to 20 minutes or until the cheese is soft and the topping is bubbly. Serve with crackers.

For a variation, substitute apricot jam, plum jam or orange marmalade for the raspberry jam.

Serves 10

Spicy Praline Cheese Spread

8 ounces cream cheese, softened
1 tablespoon grated onion
1 garlic clove, minced
1 cup pecans, finely chopped
1/4 cup packed brown sugar
1/4 cup (1/2 stick) butter or margarine
1 teaspoon Worcestershire sauce
1/2 teaspoon prepared mustard
1/2 teaspoon red pepper flakes

Mix the cream cheese, onion and garlic in a bowl. Shape into a 6-inch mound or other desired shape. Chill, covered, until firm. Combine the pecans, brown sugar, butter, Worcestershire sauce, mustard and red pepper flakes in a saucepan. Cook over medium heat until the butter and sugar are melted and the mixture is smooth, stirring frequently. Pour over the cream cheese. Chill, covered, until serving time. Serve at room temperature with crackers.

Serves 12

Sarge's Cheese Ball

16 ounces cream cheese, softened
8 ounces sharp Cheddar cheese, shredded
1 cup chopped pecans
2 garlic cloves, grated or finely chopped
1/4 cup A.1. steak sauce
1/4 teaspoon Tabasco sauce
2 tablespoons paprika

Mix the cream cheese, Cheddar cheese, pecans, garlic, steak sauce and Tabasco sauce in a bowl. Shape into a ball. Roll in the paprika and place on a serving plate. Serve with crackers.

Serves 12 to 15

Avocado and Black Bean Salsa

2 small avocados, chopped
1 (15-ounce) can black beans, rinsed
  and drained
1 small red onion, chopped
1 tablespoon chopped fresh cilantro
1½ tablespoons fresh lime juice
2 tablespoons extra-virgin olive oil
1½ teaspoons minced garlic
1 teaspoon salt or Greek seasoning

Combine the avocados, black beans, onion and cilantro in a bowl. Stir in the lime juice, olive oil, garlic and salt. Toss to combine. Serve with tortilla chips or pita chips.

Makes 2 cups

To double the shelf life of fresh cilantro, trim the stems and wrap the ends in a damp paper towel. Chill in an unsealed plastic bag.

Wedding Punch

1 (46-ounce) can pineapple juice
1½ juice cans water
2 cups sugar
3 tablespoons Fruit-Fresh
3 tablespoons red hot cinnamon candies
2 to 3 (2-liter) bottles ginger ale

Mix the pineapple juice, water, sugar and Fruit-Fresh in a large bowl. Remove 1 cup to a saucepan. Add the candies and cook until the candies have dissolved. Return to the punch. Pour into ½-gallon or 1-gallon freezer-safe containers with lids and freeze. Let stand at room temperature for 1 hour before serving. Break up with a fork and place in a punch bowl. Stir in the ginger ale and serve immediately.

Serves 50 to 75

Citrus Cooler

1 (46-ounce) can pineapple juice
1 (6-ounce) can frozen lemonade concentrate
1 (6-ounce) can frozen limeade concentrate
4 cups ginger ale
4 cups lemon-lime soda

Mix the pineapple juice, lemonade concentrate, limeade concentrate, ginger ale and soda in a large beverage urn or large pitchers.

Serves 50

Pomegranate Spritzer

8 cups pomegranate juice
2 (1-liter) bottles ginger ale or lemon-lime soda

Mix equal parts pomegranate juice and ginger ale over ice in tall glasses.

For a variation, substitute pomegranate blueberry juice or white grape juice for the pomegranate juice.

Serves 20

Sparkling Tea

4 cups water
2 family-size tea bags
1/2 cup sugar
1 (12-ounce) can frozen lemonade concentrate, thawed
4 cups water
1 (1-liter) bottle ginger ale

Bring 4 cups water to a boil in a saucepan. Remove from the heat and add the tea bags. Steep, covered, for 15 minutes. Remove and discard the tea bags. Stir in the sugar. Divide the tea, lemonade concentrate and 4 cups water among two 2-quart pitchers and mix well. Divide the ginger ale among the pitchers and mix well just before serving.

Serves 15 to 20

European Hot Chocolate

8 cups milk
4 cups half-and-half
4 cups whipping cream
2 cups sugar
6 ounces semisweet chocolate, chopped
4 teaspoons vanilla extract
Pinch of salt

Combine the milk, half-and-half, cream, sugar, chocolate, vanilla and salt in a large saucepan or stockpot. Bring to a boil, stirring constantly. Reduce the heat and simmer to keep warm while serving.

Serves 8

"Wakey, Wakey, Wakey" Eye-Opener Punch

2 cups water
$1^1/_2$ cups sugar
2 cups coffee, at room temperature
1 teaspoon vanilla extract
4 cups milk
$^1/_2$ gallon vanilla ice cream
$^1/_2$ gallon chocolate ice cream

Combine the water and sugar in a saucepan and bring to a boil. Boil for 15 minutes. Let stand until cool. Stir in the coffee and vanilla. Chill, covered, for 8 to 10 hours.

Combine the coffee mixture, milk, vanilla ice cream and chocolate ice cream in a punch bowl. Stir gently to mix. Serve immediately.

Serves 50 to 60

SARGE AT LARGE: *When traveling on Sarge's motor coach, there are many rules of the road. A speedy bathroom stop is one of them. It never fails—just as you drift off to sleep, her battle cry comes over the speaker,* "Wakey, wakey, wakey!" *Sixty people have five minutes to finish and get back into their seats. What a ride!*

Melting Pot

Being part of the Appalachian foothills, the Tennessee Valley area has a rich "melting pot" history. Early white settlers of Irish and Scottish descent began settling as early as 1805, with John Hunt at Huntsville's now famous Big Spring. A new influx of settlers began with the 1810 land sales, which brought rich English settlers who came here from Georgia and Virginia. After the Civil War, Huntsville began to expand its melting pot as northern money brought "Yankee capital" to industrialize its budding textile industry. With industrialization, Madison County became home to not only northerners, but mid-westerners and people from surrounding areas and states. Huntsville's melting pot especially grew with the twentieth century and the cold war era of rocketry. Huntsville became home to many German scientists, researchers, and young engineers from all over the world, firmly securing Huntsville's reputation as an international city of the future.

Melting Pot

Soups and Sandwiches

"Fee-esco" Taco Soup

2 pounds ground beef or chopped chicken
1 large onion, chopped
1 envelope ranch salad dressing mix
2 envelopes taco seasoning mix
2 (16-ounce) cans white corn
2 (10-ounce) cans tomatoes with green chiles
1 (16-ounce) can diced tomatoes
1 (16-ounce) can black beans
1 (16-ounce) can kidney beans
1 (16-ounce) can pinto beans
2 cups (or more) water

Brown the ground beef with the onion in a large saucepan, stirring until the ground beef is crumbly; drain. Stir in the salad dressing mix and taco seasoning mix. Add the undrained corn, undrained tomatoes with green chiles, undrained tomatoes, undrained black beans, undrained kidney beans and undrained pinto beans. Stir in the water. Simmer for 2 hours, stirring occasionally. Add additional water if the soup is too thick. Ladle into soup bowls. Garnish each serving with shredded cheese, sour cream, chopped green onions or crushed tortilla chips.

You may substitute any combination of beans.

Serves 12

Sarge at Large: *When traveling with Sarge, you can be assured you will be well taken care of. On one trip to the Magic Kingdom, the group arrived to find the hotel reservations in a bit of disarray. Sarge did her magic and handled it with a little* **"genteel persuasion."** *When she returned to the bus, she exclaimed, "You just won't believe the* **fee-esco** *(fiasco) I have just been through for you!"*

Rocket City Chili

3 slices bacon
$1^1/_2$ pounds ground chuck
1 red onion, chopped
2 garlic cloves, minced
2 (14-ounce) cans stewed tomatoes
2 (16-ounce) cans dark red kidney beans
1 (16-ounce) can pinto beans
1 (15-ounce) can Great Northern beans
1 (8-ounce) can tomato paste
1 (6-ounce) can tomato sauce
4 cups water
3 tablespoons chili powder
2 teaspoons Greek seasoning
2 teaspoons seasoned salt
1 teaspoon ground cloves
1 teaspoon seasoned pepper
$^1/_2$ teaspoon cumin

Cook the bacon in a large saucepan until crisp. Remove the bacon to paper towels to drain, reserving the drippings in the saucepan. Crumble the bacon. Brown the ground beef with the onion in the reserved drippings until the ground beef is crumbly. Add the garlic, tomatoes, kidney beans, pinto beans, Great Northern beans, tomato paste, tomato sauce and water and mix well. Stir in the bacon, chili powder, Greek seasoning, seasoned salt, cloves, seasoned pepper and cumin. Simmer for 30 minutes.

Serves 8 to 10

Sammie's Chicken Stew

1 rotisserie-cooked chicken
4 cups chicken broth
1 (15-ounce) can corn
1 (15-ounce) can diced potatoes
1 (15-ounce) can diced tomatoes
1 (15-ounce) can sliced carrots
$^1/_2$ onion, chopped
$^1/_2$ teaspoon salt, or to taste
$^1/_4$ teaspoon pepper, or to taste
16 ounces Velveeta cheese, chopped

Chop the chicken, discarding the skin and bones. Combine the chicken, broth, corn, potatoes, tomatoes, carrots, onion, salt and pepper in a large saucepan. Cook over medium heat until heated through, stirring occasionally. Add the cheese just before serving. Cook until the cheese is melted, stirring constantly.

Serves 6

Autumn Brunswick Stew

3 large chicken breasts, split into halves
10 cups water
3 potatoes, peeled and chopped
1 large onion, chopped
1/2 cup chopped celery
1 (4-pound) Boston butt pork roast,
  cooked and shredded
2 (15-ounce) cans white corn, drained
2 (15-ounce) cans cream-style corn
1 (28-ounce) can crushed tomatoes
1 (28-ounce) bottle ketchup
1/2 cup Worcestershire sauce
1/4 cup (1/2 stick) butter
2 tablespoons liquid smoke
2 teaspoons hot red pepper sauce, or to taste

Combine the chicken and water in a large heavy saucepan. Bring to a boil. Reduce the heat and simmer, covered, for 35 to 40 minutes or until the chicken is cooked through. Remove the chicken to a cutting board, reserving the cooking liquid. Chop the chicken, discarding the skin and bones. Stir the potatoes, onion and celery into the reserved cooking liquid. Bring to a boil over medium-high heat. Reduce the heat and simmer, uncovered, for 25 to 30 minutes or until the vegetables are tender. Stir in the chicken, pork, white corn, cream-style corn, tomatoes, ketchup, Worcestershire sauce, butter, liquid smoke and hot sauce. Simmer, uncovered, for 1 hour.

Serves 15 to 20

Creamy Mexican Chicken and Corn Chowder

2 chicken bouillon cubes
1 cup hot water
$1^1/_2$ pounds boneless chicken breasts, chopped
$^1/_2$ cup chopped onion
1 teaspoon minced garlic
3 tablespoons butter
1 teaspoon cumin
1 (20-ounce) tube frozen cream-style corn
2 cups half-and-half
1 (10-ounce) can tomatoes with green chiles
1 (4-ounce) can diced green chiles
$^1/_2$ to 1 teaspoon hot red pepper sauce
8 ounces Monterey Jack cheese, shredded

Dissolve the bouillon cubes in the hot water. Brown the chicken with the onion and garlic in the butter in a large heavy saucepan. Stir in the bouillon and cumin. Bring to a boil. Add the corn and simmer until the corn is thawed, stirring occasionally. Stir in the half-and-half, tomatoes with green chiles, green chiles and hot sauce. Cook over low heat until heated through. Add the cheese and cook until the cheese melts, stirring constantly. Garnish with crushed tortilla chips. Serve immediately.

Serves 6

Yankee Bean Soup

8 ounces dried navy beans
5 cups water
2 ounces salt pork, cut into cubes
$^1/_3$ cup sliced onion (cut into rings)
1 teaspoon molasses
$^1/_2$ teaspoon salt, or to taste
3 slices bacon, chopped
$^1/_4$ cup chopped onion
$1^1/_2$ cups chopped carrots
$^1/_3$ cup finely chopped celery leaves
2 cups milk or fat-free half-and-half

Combine the beans and water in a saucepan. Bring to a boil. Remove from the heat and let stand for 2 hours or longer. Stir in the pork, sliced onion, molasses and $^1/_2$ teaspoon salt. Simmer for 2 hours or until the beans are tender, stirring occasionally. Sauté the bacon, chopped onion, carrots and celery leaves in a skillet until the bacon is crisp. Mash the beans slightly and return to the soup. Stir in the bacon mixture and milk. Adjust the seasonings to taste. Simmer for 10 minutes, stirring occasionally; do not boil.

Serves 6

I-Can't-Believe-It's-Low-Fat Broccoli Cheese Soup

1 head broccoli, cut into crowns
1 cup fat-free low-sodium chicken broth
Spray butter
1 teaspoon lemon pepper
1/3 cup all-purpose flour
2 1/4 cups fat-free half-and-half
2 1/2 cups fat-free low-sodium chicken broth
2 (10-ounce) cans low-fat cream of chicken soup
12 ounces light Velveeta cheese, chopped
Salt and pepper to taste

Combine the broccoli and 1 cup broth in a large saucepan. Spray the tops of the broccoli with four or five sprays of spray butter and sprinkle with the lemon pepper. Bring to a boil. Boil until most of the liquid has evaporated. Remove the broccoli with a slotted spoon to a cutting board. Chop and set aside. Add the flour to the saucepan. Whisk in the half-and-half. Cook over medium heat for 5 minutes or until thickened, whisking constantly. Add 2 1/2 cups broth, the soup and cheese. Cook until the cheese melts, stirring frequently. Stir in the broccoli. Season with salt and pepper.

Serves 6

French Onion Soup

3 pounds sweet onions or white onions, thinly sliced
3/4 cup (1 1/2 sticks) butter
1 tablespoon all-purpose flour
5 (10-ounce) cans beef broth
1 cup red wine
1/2 teaspoon dried thyme
1/2 teaspoon pepper
2 cups (8 ounces) shredded Muenster cheese
2 cups (8 ounces) shredded Swiss cheese
1 1/2 cups (6 ounces) shredded Parmesan cheese
8 slices French bread, toasted

Cook the onions in the butter in a large saucepan over medium heat for 40 minutes, stirring frequently. Add the flour and cook for 2 minutes, stirring constantly. Stir in the broth, wine, thyme and pepper. Bring to a boil. Reduce the heat and simmer, covered, for 30 minutes. Mix the Muenster cheese, Swiss cheese and Parmesan cheese in a bowl. Place each slice of bread in an ovenproof soup bowl sprayed with nonstick cooking spray. Ladle the soup over the bread. Sprinkle with the cheese mixture. Broil until the cheese is melted.

Serves 8

Potato Leek Soup

2 bunches leeks (6 to 8)
8 slices bacon, chopped
6 ribs celery, chopped
4 potatoes, peeled and chopped
8 cups chicken broth
2 teaspoons salt
3 cups cream or fat-free half-and-half
1 cup milk

Remove and discard the tough dark green parts and the root bottom of the leeks. Wash the leeks thoroughly, removing all the grit. Slice into 1/2-inch pieces. Sauté the bacon in a large saucepan until the drippings are translucent. Add the leeks and celery. Cook, covered, for 10 minutes. Add the potatoes, broth and salt. Cook until the potatoes are tender. Let stand until cool. Process in batches in a blender or with an immersion blender until well blended. Stir in the cream and milk. Cook until heated through.

For a variation, slice 1/2 to 1 package smoked or Polish sausage into 1/2-inch pieces. Brown in a skillet with the milk and cream before adding to the soup.

Serves 8 to 10

Highland's Tomato Basil Soup

1 onion, chopped
3 carrots, chopped
2 to 3 tablespoons olive oil
1 (28-ounce) can plum tomatoes,
or 8 to 10 plum tomatoes, chopped
2 cups water
1 teaspoon salt
1 teaspoon freshly ground pepper
1/2 cup orange juice
1 to 2 cups heavy cream or fat-free half-and-half
4 fresh basil leaves, chopped

Sauté the onion and carrots in the olive oil in a heavy stockpot. Add the tomatoes, water, salt and pepper. Bring to a boil. Stir in the orange juice. Reduce the heat and simmer for 10 to 15 minutes. Process in a blender or with an immersion blender until smooth. Stir in the cream and basil. Cook until heated through; do not boil.

Serves 4 to 6

Italian Beef on Toasted Deli Rolls

4 pounds boneless rump roast or sirloin tip roast,
cut into 1/4-inch-thick slices
2 envelopes au jus gravy mix
4 cups (or more) water
2 tablespoons Italian seasoning
1 tablespoon paprika
1 large bay leaf, or 2 small bay leaves
2 teaspoons garlic powder
1 package kaiser rolls

Place the beef in a large heavy saucepan. Mix the gravy mix, water, Italian seasoning, paprika, bay leaf and garlic powder in a bowl. Pour over the beef. Bring to a boil. Reduce the heat and simmer, covered, for 45 minutes or until the beef is very tender. Add additional water if needed. Remove and discard the bay leaf. Serve on the rolls. Serve with sour cream and potato chips.

Serves 8 to 12

Baked Ham Sandwiches with Jezebel Sauce

Jezebel Sauce
1 cup pineapple preserves
1 cup apple jelly or apricot jelly
1 (3-ounce) jar prepared mustard
6 ounces freshly prepared horseradish
Salt and pepper to taste

Sandwiches
8 hamburger buns
8 slices cooked ham
8 slices Swiss cheese

For the sauce, beat the pineapple preserves, apple jelly, mustard and horseradish in a mixing bowl. Season with salt and pepper.

For the sandwiches, spread the sauce over the cut sides of the buns. Place one slice of ham and one slice of cheese on each bottom bun. Top each with a top bun. Wrap each sandwich in foil. Place directly on the oven rack and bake at 450 degrees for 15 minutes.

For Baked Ham Sandwiches with Poppy Seed Mustard Sauce, mix 1/4 cup softened butter, 1 tablespoon mayonnaise, 2 tablespoons prepared mustard, 2 tablespoons chopped onion and 1 1/2 teaspoons poppy seeds in a bowl. Substitute for the Jezebel Sauce.

Serves 8

"Peek-You-Up" Panini

12 ounces thinly sliced pancetta
6 tablespoons extra-virgin olive oil
1/2 cup packed torn basil leaves
2 teaspoons dried oregano
1/2 teaspoon salt
Pepper to taste
6 Campari tomatoes, thickly sliced
12 thin slices whole grain bread, lightly toasted
6 slices provolone cheese
4 cups baby arugula or mixed greens
4 to 6 tablespoons butter, softened

Sauté the pancetta in batches in a skillet over medium heat for 6 minutes or until crisp and brown. Drain on paper towels. Combine the olive oil, basil, oregano, salt and pepper in a shallow dish. Add the tomatoes, turning to coat. Let stand for 30 to 60 minutes. Place six slices of the bread on a work surface. Layer each with one slice of cheese, one slice of tomato, the pancetta, arugula and one slice of bread. Butter both sides of the sandwiches and grill in a panini press or grill pan until the cheese begins to melt and the bread is brown.

Serves 6

Sarge at Large: *One thing you must be aware of on a Sarge trip is time. If you are not present at the designated departure site on time, she will leave you. You will have to call a cab to come* "peek-you-up"! *The lesson is not to be late.*

Day-After-Thanksgiving Bake

$1\frac{1}{3}$ cups chopped turkey
$\frac{1}{2}$ cup (2 ounces) shredded Cheddar cheese
$\frac{1}{4}$ cup mayonnaise
8 slices bread, crusts trimmed
3 eggs
1 cup milk
$\frac{1}{8}$ teaspoon celery salt
$\frac{1}{8}$ teaspoon seasoned salt

Mix the turkey, cheese and mayonnaise in a bowl. Spread over four slices of the bread and top each with a slice of the remaining bread. Place the sandwiches in a single layer in a buttered square baking pan. Mix the eggs and milk in a bowl. Pour over the sandwiches. Sprinkle with the celery salt and seasoned salt. Chill, covered, for 8 to 10 hours. Bake at 350 degrees for 45 minutes.

Serves 4

Baked Chicken Salad Sandwiches

3 cups chopped cooked chicken breast
1 cup chopped celery
2 hard-cooked eggs, chopped
$\frac{1}{2}$ cup mayonnaise
Salt and pepper to taste
12 thin slices sandwich bread, crusts trimmed
1 cup sour cream
1 (10-ounce) can cream of chicken soup
6 ounces potato chips, crushed

Mix the chicken, celery, eggs and mayonnaise in a bowl. Season with salt and pepper. Spread over one side of six slices of the bread and top each with a slice of the remaining bread. Place the sandwiches in a single layer in a buttered 9×13-inch baking dish. Mix the sour cream and soup in a bowl. Spread over the tops of the sandwiches. Chill, covered, for 8 to 10 hours. Let stand at room temperature for 30 minutes. Sprinkle with the chips. Bake at 325 degrees for 40 to 45 minutes.

Serves 6

Chicken French Bread

1 loaf French bread
Softened butter
1 (12-ounce) can chicken, drained
1/2 cup sour cream
1/2 cup mayonnaise
2 tablespoons chopped parsley
1/8 teaspoon garlic salt
2 cups (8 ounces) shredded Cheddar cheese

Slice the bread horizontally into halves. Spread the cut sides of both halves with butter. Mix the chicken, sour cream, mayonnaise, parsley and garlic salt in a bowl. Spread over the buttered bread. Place crust side down on a baking sheet. Sprinkle with the cheese. Bake at 350 degrees until the cheese melts and the bread is crisp. Slice each half into three pieces. This may be frozen until baking time.

Serves 6

Artichoke "Ought-a-Choke" Bread

1 tablespoon minced garlic
2 teaspoons sesame seeds
1/4 cup (1/2 stick) butter
1 (14-ounce) can artichoke hearts, drained and chopped
1 cup (4 ounces) shredded Monterey Jack cheese
1 cup (4 ounces) grated Parmesan cheese
1/2 cup sour cream
1 (16-ounce) loaf French bread
1/2 cup (2 ounces) shredded Cheddar cheese

Sauté the garlic and sesame seeds in the butter in a skillet until light brown. Remove from the heat and stir in the artichokes, Monterey Jack cheese, Parmesan cheese and sour cream. Slice the bread horizontally into halves. Hollow out the centers, leaving 1-inch shells. Crumble the bread and stir into the artichoke mixture. Spoon into the bread shells and place on a baking sheet. Sprinkle with the Cheddar cheese. Cover with foil. Bake at 350 degrees for 25 minutes. Bake, uncovered, for 5 minutes longer or until the cheese is melted. Cut into twelve slices. This may be frozen before being baked.

Serves 12

SARGE AT LARGE: "Ought-a-choke" *is what you may want to do to Sarge after being on a one-week motor coach trip!*

Dixie Pimento Cheese

8 ounces sharp Cheddar cheese, finely shredded
8 ounces mild Cheddar cheese, finely shredded
8 ounces Velveeta cheese, finely shredded
1/2 to 1 cup mayonnaise
1 (4-ounce) jar sliced pimentos, mashed
1 teaspoon Tabasco sauce
1 teaspoon prepared mustard
1 teaspoon pepper
1/2 teaspoon salt, or to taste
1/4 teaspoon minced garlic

Mix the sharp Cheddar cheese, mild Cheddar cheese and Velveeta cheese in a bowl. Let stand to come to room temperature. Add the mayonnaise, pimentos, Tabasco sauce, mustard, pepper, salt and garlic. Mix by hand. Chill, covered, until serving time. Use for sandwiches.

Serves 6 to 8

South-of-the-Border Cheese Spread

1 1/2 cups mayonnaise
8 ounces extra-sharp Cheddar cheese, shredded
8 ounces sharp Cheddar cheese, shredded
1 tablespoon grated onion
1 (4-ounce) jar diced pimentos, drained
1/2 cup chopped jalapeño chiles
1 teaspoon Worcestershire sauce

Mix the mayonnaise, extra-sharp Cheddar cheese, sharp Cheddar cheese, onion, pimentos, jalapeño chiles and Worcestershire sauce in a bowl. Chill, covered, until serving time. Use for sandwiches.

Serves 8

Fields of Green

Long before John Hunt came to the Big Spring, the Cherokee and Chickasaw Indians were enjoying the wonderful wild "cress" that grew in the cold limestone springs in north Madison County.

It wasn't until Dennis Watercress Company opened in 1915 that Huntsville was named the Watercress Capital of the World. Watercress was shipped in wooden barrels up the East Coast to fine restaurants and hotels. The famous Waldorf Astoria Hotel in New York City and the Whitehouse in Washington, D.C., served Madison County's watercress to dignitaries, kings, and queens from around the world. Noted for its peppery, zesty flavor, watercress, "The Health Food from America," contains more vitamin C than orange juice, more vitamin A than broccoli, and more calcium than a glass of whole milk. It also possesses cancer-suppressing properties.

Photo: 1955

Mrs. Jimmy Taylor (Katherine) and Mr. John Ward being served watercress salad at the Russel Erskine Hotel by headwaiter Jack Byrne.

Fields of Green

Watercress Capital of the World

Watercress Salad

2 cups watercress, torn
4 scallions, chopped
4 slices bacon, crisp-cooked and crumbled
1 head leaf lettuce
1/2 recipe French Dressing (below)

Toss the watercress, scallions and bacon in a bowl. Arrange a bed of lettuce on each of four salad plates. Spoon the watercress mixture over the top. Serve with the French Dressing.

Serves 4

French Dressing

1/2 cup sugar
1/4 cup balsamic vinegar
1 garlic clove, minced
1 tablespoon chopped onion
1 teaspoon Worcestershire sauce
1 teaspoon dry mustard
1 teaspoon paprika
1 teaspoon Greek seasoning
1 teaspoon parsley
1 teaspoon poppy seeds
1 teaspoon salt
1/2 cup olive oil
1/2 cup canola oil
1/2 cup crumbled blue cheese

Combine the sugar, vinegar, garlic, onion and Worcestershire sauce in a blender. Add the mustard, paprika, Greek seasoning, parsley, poppy seeds and salt. Process until mixed. Add the olive oil and canola oil in a fine stream, processing constantly at high speed until smooth. Add the cheese and process at low speed just until mixed. Chill, covered, until serving time.

Serves 8

Greek "God-dest" Salad with Sun-Dried Tomatoes and Bacon

1/2 cup white wine vinegar or red wine vinegar
2 cups vegetable oil
1 large onion, sliced into thin rings
1 head cauliflower, cut into florets
1 (4-ounce) jar sliced olives, drained
2 heads lettuce, torn
Crumbled blue cheese to taste
4 slices bacon, crisp-cooked and crumbled
1/4 cup oil-pack sun-dried tomatoes, drained
2 teaspoons Greek seasoning
Freshly ground pepper to taste

Pour the vinegar into a bowl. Add the oil in a fine stream, whisking constantly until mixed. Add the onion, cauliflower and olives. Toss to coat. Chill, covered, for 8 to 10 hours. Combine the lettuce, cheese and onion mixture in a large serving bowl. Toss to mix. Sprinkle with the bacon, sun-dried tomatoes and Greek seasoning. Season with pepper.

Serves 10 to 12

Sarge at Large: *Traveling through Birmingham, the motor coach zoomed past the great Vulcan statue on Red Mountain. Sarge looked up and said, "He is the* God-dest *of fire and was made of iron." I am sure it was just a slip of the tongue, but it delighted one and all.*

Spinach Salad with Hot Bacon Dressing and Candied Pecans

Candied Pecans

1 egg white
3/4 cup packed light brown sugar
1 teaspoon vanilla extract
2 cups pecan halves

Hot Bacon Dressing

12 ounces bacon, chopped
1/2 cup chopped onion
2 cups water
1 cup cider vinegar
1 1/2 cups sugar
2 tablespoons Dijon mustard
1 teaspoon salt
1/4 teaspoon pepper
3 tablespoons cornstarch
2 tablespoons cold water

Salad

7 ounces spinach leaves
1 (8-ounce) can mandarin oranges, drained

For the pecans, beat the egg white in a mixing bowl until stiff peaks form. Fold in the brown sugar gradually. Fold in the vanilla. Add the pecans gradually, coating well. Arrange the pecans on a greased baking sheet. Do not let the pecans touch. Bake at 250 degrees for 30 minutes.

For the dressing, cook the bacon in a large skillet until crisp. Remove the bacon to paper towels to drain, reserving the drippings in the skillet. Sauté the onion in the reserved drippings until tender. Remove from the heat and stir in 2 cups water, the vinegar, sugar, Dijon mustard, salt, pepper and bacon. Mix the cornstarch and 2 tablespoons cold water in a small bowl. Stir into the bacon mixture. Bring to a boil over medium heat. Boil for 2 minutes, stirring constantly.

To assemble the salad, combine the spinach and mandarin oranges in a serving bowl. Pour the hot dressing over the top and sprinkle with the candied pecans.

Serves 4

Marinated Asparagus and Hearts of Palm Salad

3 pounds asparagus
3/4 cup vegetable oil
1/2 cup cider vinegar
3 garlic cloves, crushed
1 1/2 teaspoons salt
1 teaspoon pepper
2 (14-ounce) cans hearts of palm, drained and
cut into 1/2-inch slices
1 pint cherry tomatoes or grape tomatoes
1 head Bibb lettuce

Snap off the woody ends of the asparagus spears. Steam until tender; drain. Combine the oil, vinegar, garlic, salt and pepper in a jar with a tight-fitting lid and seal tightly. Shake to mix. Combine the asparagus, hearts of palm, tomatoes and vinegar mixture in a sealable plastic bag. Chill, tightly sealed, for 8 hours, turning occasionally. Drain, discarding the marinade. Serve over a bed of the lettuce.

For a variation, add sliced black olives, chopped red bell pepper, chopped cucumber, chopped celery and chopped onion.

Serves 12

Triple Bean Salad

1 (10-ounce) package frozen French-style green beans
1 (10-ounce) package frozen baby lima beans
1 (10-ounce) package frozen green peas
1 cup mayonnaise
2 hard-cooked eggs, chopped
3 tablespoons lemon juice
2 tablespoons minced onion
1 teaspoon Worcestershire sauce
1 teaspoon prepared mustard
1/4 teaspoon garlic salt
Dash of hot red pepper sauce
1 (3-ounce) package slivered almonds, toasted

Cook the green beans, lima beans and peas according to the package directions until tender. Drain and combine in a bowl. Add the mayonnaise, eggs, lemon juice, onion, Worcestershire sauce, mustard, garlic salt and hot sauce. Toss to mix. Sprinkle with the almonds.

Serves 8

Christmas Coleslaw

20 ounces shredded cabbage
1/2 green bell pepper, chopped
1/2 red bell pepper, chopped
1 onion, chopped
1 cup sugar
1/2 cup plus 2 tablespoons
  apple cider vinegar
1/2 cup vegetable oil
1 teaspoon salt
1 teaspoon celery seeds

Mix the cabbage, green bell pepper, red bell pepper, onion and sugar in a bowl. Chill, covered, for 2 hours. Combine the vinegar, oil, salt and celery seeds in a saucepan. Bring to a boil, stirring constantly until the salt dissolves. Let stand until cool. Pour over the cabbage mixture and toss gently to coat. Chill, covered, for 2 hours.

Serves 8 to 10

This is a colorful coleslaw to serve any time of the year.

New Potato Salad

2 1/2 pounds unpeeled red potatoes, chopped
4 garlic cloves, chopped
2 tablespoons olive oil
Salt to taste
1 cup mayonnaise
1/4 cup brown horseradish mustard
1 bunch green onions, chopped
1 cup crumbled crisp-cooked bacon
3 hard-cooked eggs, chopped

Combine the potatoes, garlic and olive oil in a bowl. Toss to coat. Spread out on a baking sheet. Season with salt. Bake at 450 degrees for 30 minutes, tossing occasionally. Let stand until cool. Mix the mayonnaise and mustard in a bowl. Add the potato mixture, green onions, bacon and eggs. Toss to mix. Chill, covered, until serving time.

Serves 8

Loaded Potato Salad

5 pounds red potatoes
1 bunch green onions, chopped
1 bunch fresh parsley, chopped
1 (4-ounce) package bacon bits
1 cup sour cream
1/2 to 1 cup mayonnaise
1/4 cup sugar
Salt and pepper to taste
1/2 cup (2 ounces) shredded
Cheddar cheese

Combine the potatoes with enough water to cover in a large saucepan. Bring to a boil and boil just until fork-tender; drain. Let the potatoes stand to cool. Chop the potatoes and place in a large bowl. Add the green onions, parsley, bacon, sour cream, mayonnaise and sugar. Stir to mix. Season with salt and pepper. Chill, covered, until serving time. Sprinkle with the cheese just before serving.

Serves 12

Caprese Salad with White Balsamic Basil Vinaigrette

White Balsamic Basil Vinaigrette

1/2 cup white balsamic vinegar
2 to 3 tablespoons chopped
fresh basil
2 tablespoons fresh lemon juice
1 teaspoon Dijon mustard
1 teaspoon sugar
1/2 teaspoon minced garlic
1/2 teaspoon salt
1/2 teaspoon pepper
1/3 cup canola oil or olive oil

Salad

Mixed salad greens
4 tomatoes, peeled and sliced
4 to 6 ounces fresh mozzarella
cheese, sliced, or crumbled
feta cheese

For the vinaigrette, process the vinegar, basil, lemon juice, Dijon mustard, sugar, garlic, salt and pepper in a food processor or blender until mixed. Add the canola oil in a fine stream, processing constantly until smooth.

For the salad, toss salad greens with vinaigrette to taste in a bowl just before serving. Top with the tomatoes and cheese.

Serves 4 to 6

Tomato Olive Salad

$1\frac{1}{2}$ (10-ounce) cans tomato soup
8 ounces cream cheese, chopped
1 envelope unflavored gelatin
1 cup mayonnaise
1 cup chopped pecans, toasted
$\frac{1}{2}$ cup chopped celery
$\frac{1}{4}$ cup chopped green onions
1 (4-ounce) can sliced olives, drained
1 tablespoon chopped green bell pepper

Combine the soup and cream cheese in a saucepan. Cook until the cream cheese is melted, stirring frequently. Soften the gelatin in a small amount of cold water. Stir into the soup mixture and remove from the heat. Add the mayonnaise, pecans, celery, green onions, olives and bell pepper and mix well. Pour into an 8×8-inch glass baking dish or mold. Chill until firm. Slice to serve.

Serves 12

Corn Bread Salad

$\frac{1}{2}$ cup pickle relish
1 (8-ounce) package corn bread mix
9 to 12 slices bacon, crisp-cooked and crumbled
2 tomatoes, chopped
1 bell pepper, chopped
1 onion, chopped
1 cup mayonnaise
Celery salt to taste
Pepper to taste

Drain the pickle relish, reserving $\frac{1}{4}$ cup of the pickle juice. Prepare the corn bread mix according to the package directions for a 9-inch pan, adding 2 tablespoons of the pickle juice. Let cool and crumble. Mix the bacon, tomatoes, bell pepper, onion and pickle relish in a bowl. Mix the mayonnaise and the remaining 2 tablespoons pickle juice in a bowl. Layer the corn bread, celery salt, pepper, tomato mixture and mayonnaise mixture one-half at a time in a large serving dish. Chill, covered, until serving time.

Serves 10

For a festive presentation, layer in a clean terra-cotta plant saucer.

Avocado Chicken Salad

4 ounces mushrooms, sliced
1 tablespoon butter
1/2 cup chopped pecans, toasted
1/2 cup chopped celery
1 (10-ounce) can cream of celery soup
1/4 cup mayonnaise
3 tablespoons lemon juice
2 teaspoons Dijon mustard
2 teaspoons sugar (optional)
Dash of salt
Dash of pepper
5 cups chopped cooked chicken
1 avocado, sliced
Juice of 1 lemon
1 bunch lettuce leaves
2 tomatoes, cut into wedges

Sauté the mushrooms in the butter in a skillet until tender. Mix the pecans, celery, soup, mayonnaise, 3 tablespoons lemon juice, the Dijon mustard, sugar, salt and pepper in a bowl. Stir in the chicken and mushrooms. Dip the avocado slices in lemon juice and chill, covered, until needed.

To assemble, spoon the chicken salad onto lettuce-lined plates. Place the avocado and tomatoes around the chicken salad.

Serves 6

Covington's Signature Chicken Salad

4 pounds split bone-in chicken breasts (about 8)
2 chicken bouillon cubes
8 hard-cooked eggs, chopped
4 ribs celery, chopped
1 cup red seedless grape halves
1 tablespoon parsley flakes
1 teaspoon salt
1 teaspoon coarsely ground pepper
2 cups mayonnaise
1 teaspoon chicken bouillon paste

Boil the chicken with the bouillon cubes in enough water to cover in a large saucepan or stockpot until the chicken is cooked through and tender; drain. Chop the chicken, discarding the bones and skin. Place the chicken in a bowl and chill. Add the eggs, celery, grapes, parsley, salt and pepper to the chicken. Toss to mix. Mix the mayonnaise with the bouillon paste in a bowl. Fold into the chicken mixture. Chill, covered, until serving time.

Serves 12 to 15

Covington's Downtown is located in the heart of Huntsville. Their signature chicken salad has been served in their café since their opening day, February 13, 1989.

Kenny Mango's Lemon Curry Chicken Salad

1/2 cup chopped walnuts, toasted
1 tablespoon mild curry powder
1 teaspoon salt
1 teaspoon pepper
3/4 cup mayonnaise
1/2 cup sour cream
1/2 cup chopped celery
1/2 cup red or purple grape halves
2 tablespoons lemon juice
32 ounces canned all-white-meat chicken, drained, or 4 cups chopped cooked chicken

Mix the walnuts, curry powder, salt and pepper in a bowl. Stir in the mayonnaise, sour cream, celery, grapes and lemon juice. Fold in the chicken. Chill, covered, for 6 hours. Serve over a bed of lettuce or as a sandwich on a sliced croissant.

Serves 6

Kenny Mango's Coffee Shop opened in September 2004 on the north side of Huntsville's downtown square. The coffee shop moved in 2007 to Madison Market shopping center on Hughes Road, where wonderful coffees, smoothies, and cappuccinos, along with delicious chicken salad, are served in a colonial Caribbean atmosphere.

Shrimp and Feta Pasta Salad

16 ounces bow tie pasta
1 sweet onion, chopped
1/2 large red bell pepper, chopped
1/2 green bell pepper, chopped
2 ribs celery, chopped
3 garlic cloves, minced
1 tablespoon butter
1 tablespoon vegetable oil
Salt and pepper to taste
1 pound medium shrimp
1 (14-ounce) can quartered artichokes, drained and chopped
1 (6-ounce) can large black olives, sliced
1 (8-ounce) bottle Italian salad dressing
6 ounces feta cheese, crumbled

Cook the pasta according to the package directions; drain. Sauté the onion, red bell pepper, green bell pepper, celery and garlic in the butter and oil in a skillet until tender. Season with salt and pepper. Add the shrimp, artichokes, olives and salad dressing. Sauté until the shrimp turn pink. Combine the pasta and the shrimp mixture in a bowl and toss to mix. Chill, covered, until serving time. Sprinkle with the cheese just before serving.

Serves 4

French "Chat-ow" Herb Vinaigrette

1/2 cup extra-virgin olive oil
3 tablespoons white wine vinegar
1/2 teaspoon prepared mustard
1 garlic clove, finely chopped or pressed
2 teaspoons herbes de Provence
1/4 teaspoon salt
1/8 teaspoon pepper
Sugar or sugar substitute to taste

Combine the olive oil, vinegar, mustard, garlic, herbes de Provence, salt, pepper and sugar in a jar with a tight-fitting lid and seal tightly. Shake to mix. Adjust the seasonings to taste. Chill until serving time. Let stand at room temperature for 30 minutes before serving. Shake well before serving.

Makes 1 cup

Sarge at Large: *At the Biltmore, Sarge had so much information to impart before going on the tour of the mansion. "This is an excellent example of a French* chat-ow *(chateau)." She might not pronounce it correctly, but you can be assured she's got the information correct!*

Roquefort Dressing

8 ounces Roquefort cheese, crumbled
4 cups mayonnaise
1 (12-ounce) can evaporated milk
1 (8-ounce) bottle Italian salad dressing
1 tablespoon lemon juice
Dash of Tabasco sauce
Dash of Worcestershire sauce
Salt and pepper to taste

Mix the cheese and mayonnaise in a bowl. Whisk in the evaporated milk, salad dressing, lemon juice, Tabasco sauce and Worcestershire sauce. Season with salt and pepper. Chill, covered, until serving time.

Makes 6 cups

Main Event

Huntsville native Tallulah Bankhead was the toast of the London theater in the 1920s and became nationally renowned for her dramatic roles. She appeared in **The Little Foxes** *(1939),* **The Skin of Our Teeth** *(1942), the movie* **Lifeboat** *(1944), and as emcee of* **The Big Show** *on NBC radio (1950–1952).*

She was born in Huntsville on January 31, 1902, in an upstairs apartment of the I. Schiffman Building on the east side of the courthouse square in Huntsville. Her father, William Brockman Bankhead, was then Huntsville's City Attorney, and later became Speaker of the U.S. House of Representatives. She is named for her paternal grandmother, Tallulah Brockman Bankhead. A ravishing beauty in her youth, Tallulah was known for her uninhibited exuberance, deep sultry voice, and calling everyone "Dahling." She appeared in fifty-six plays, nineteen movies, and scores of radio and television productions during her fifty-year career. She was but a spark in the fire of the growing arts in Huntsville.

Main Event

Stars of the Show

"Ta-lee-la" (Tallulah) Tilapia with Scallion Sauce

4 tilapia fillets
1/4 cup all-purpose flour
Salt to taste
Pepper to taste
3 tablespoons olive oil
1/2 cup chicken stock
1 tablespoon lemon juice
1 tablespoon butter, melted
1 garlic clove, minced
3 scallions, chopped

Dredge the tilapia in the flour, shaking off any excess. Season with salt and pepper. Cook in the olive oil in a skillet for 4 to 6 minutes or until the fish are brown and begin to flake, turning once. Remove to a plate and keep warm, reserving the drippings in the skillet. Mix the stock, lemon juice, butter and garlic in a bowl. Add to the reserved drippings. Cook until the liquid is reduced by one-half, stirring constantly and scraping up any brown bits from the bottom of the skillet. Add the scallions and cook for 10 seconds, stirring constantly. Pour over the fish and serve immediately.

Serves 4

Sarge at Large: *On a tour of Huntsville with Madison Academy's third grade, Sarge talked about the history of downtown. As she passed the Schiffman building on the square, she explained that the upstairs apartment was the birthplace of the famous actress "Ta-lee-la" (Tallulah) Bankhead. Tallulah would have said to Sarge in her sultry voice, "That's perfectly all right, Dahling!"*

Asian "Snappers"

4 (6-ounce) red snapper fillets, halibut fillets
or grouper fillets
1/2 cup dry sherry
3 tablespoons low-sodium soy sauce
1 tablespoon sugar
1/2 cup sliced green onions

Heat a skillet over medium-high heat and coat with garlic flavor nonstick cooking spray. Add the fish. Cook for 8 minutes or until the fish begins to flake, turning once. Remove to a plate and keep warm, reserving the drippings in the skillet. Mix the sherry, soy sauce and sugar in a bowl. Pour into the hot skillet and cook for 2 minutes or until thickened, stirring constantly and scraping up any brown bits from the bottom of the skillet. Return the fish to the skillet and turn gently to coat with the sauce. Sprinkle with the green onions. This dish is excellent served with jasmine rice and steamed broccoli.

Serves 4

Sarge at Large: *Sarge makes an annual spring pilgrimage to Washington, D.C., with the Madison Academy fifth graders and their parents. On one hilarious trip, she pointed out the "snappers" (snipers) perched on top of the White House. Everyone was puzzled as to why there were fish on the top of the executive residence.*

Grilled Salmon with Kiwifruit-Mango Salsa

Kiwifruit-Mango Salsa
1 cup chopped kiwifruit
3/4 cup chopped mango
3 tablespoons finely chopped red onion
1/2 teaspoon freshly grated ginger
1/4 teaspoon salt
1 tablespoon fresh lime juice
2 teaspoons extra-virgin olive oil

Salmon
1 teaspoon canola oil
1 teaspoon freshly grated ginger
1 tablespoon fresh lime juice
1 small jalapeño chile, seeded and minced
Salt and pepper to taste
1 pound salmon steaks

For the salsa, combine the kiwifruit, mango, onion, ginger, salt, lime juice and olive oil in a bowl and mix well.

For the salmon, mix the canola oil, ginger, lime juice, jalapeño chile, salt and pepper in a nonreactive bowl. Add the salmon and turn to coat. Chill, covered, for 1 to 2 hours. Drain the salmon, discarding the marinade. Place skin side down on a grill rack. Grill for 4 to 5 minutes or until the salmon begins to flake. Serve the salsa over the salmon.

For a variation, substitute tuna steaks for the salmon.

Serves 4

Honey-Curry-Glazed Salmon

4 (6-ounce) salmon fillets
3/4 cup honey
4 teaspoons Dijon mustard
2 1/2 teaspoons curry powder
1/2 teaspoon sea salt
1/2 teaspoon freshly ground pepper

Place the salmon skin side down on a broiler pan sprayed with nonstick cooking spray. Mix the honey, Dijon mustard, curry powder, salt and pepper in a small bowl until smooth. Brush over the salmon. Broil for 8 to 10 minutes or until the salmon begins to flake.

Serves 4

Bayou Baked Shrimp

1/4 cup (1/2 stick) butter, melted
1 (8-ounce) bottle Italian salad dressing
Juice of 2 lemons
1 tablespoon (or less) pepper
3 pounds large shrimp, peeled and deveined

Mix the butter, salad dressing, lemon juice and pepper in a 9×13-inch baking dish. Add the shrimp and toss to coat. Bake at 325 degrees for 25 to 30 minutes, stirring frequently.

Serves 6 to 8

Shrimp and Artichoke Bake

1 (10-ounce) package frozen chopped spinach, thawed and drained
1 (14-ounce) can artichokes, drained
1 cup heavy cream
2 cups (8 ounces) grated Parmesan cheese
2 pounds bulk pork sausage
2 cups small shrimp
1/2 cup white wine
1/4 cup (1/2 stick) butter
1 cup (4 ounces) shredded smoked Gouda cheese

Combine the spinach and artichokes in a saucepan. Cook until heated through, stirring occasionally. Add the cream and cook until thickened, stirring constantly. Stir in the Parmesan cheese and remove from the heat.

Brown the sausage in a skillet, stirring until crumbly; drain. Sauté the shrimp in the wine and butter in a skillet until the shrimp turn pink; drain. Mix the spinach mixture, sausage and shrimp in a bowl. Spoon into a 9×13-inch baking dish and sprinkle with the Gouda cheese. Bake at 350 degrees until the cheese is melted and the top is brown.

Serves 12

Smoky Shrimp with Peppers and Creamy Cheese Grits

6 ounces Canadian bacon, chopped
1 cup red bell pepper strips
1 cup green bell pepper strips
1 (14-ounce) can tomatoes with
green chiles, drained
$1^1/_2$ pounds medium shrimp, peeled and deveined
$^1/_2$ cup chopped green onions
Salt and pepper to taste
$1^2/_3$ cups fat-free half-and-half
2 cups chicken broth
1 cup quick-cooking grits
1 cup (4 ounces) shredded Cheddar cheese or
Gouda cheese

Sauté the Canadian bacon in a skillet until light brown. Add the red bell pepper and green bell pepper. Cook for 10 minutes, stirring occasionally. Add the tomatoes with green chiles and cook for 5 minutes, stirring occasionally. Add the shrimp and cook for 3 minutes or until the shrimp turn pink, stirring frequently. Stir in the green onions and season with salt and pepper. Keep warm.

Combine the half-and-half and broth in a saucepan. Bring to a boil. Add the grits gradually, stirring constantly. Return to a boil. Reduce the heat and simmer for 5 minutes or until thickened, stirring occasionally. Stir in the cheese. Spoon onto plates or into shallow bowls. Spoon the shrimp mixture over the grits.

Serves 4

Rotisserie Chicken with Artichokes and Roasted Red Pepper Alfredo

1 rotisserie-cooked chicken
1 red onion, chopped
1 tablespoon olive oil
2 tablespoons brown sugar
1 (14-ounce) can diced tomatoes with garlic
1 (16-ounce) jar roasted red pepper Alfredo sauce
1 (15-ounce) can quartered artichokes, drained
1 teaspoon Cavender's Greek seasoning
1 teaspoon freshly ground pepper
Hot cooked rice or pasta

Chop the chicken, discarding the bones and skin. Sauté the onion in the olive oil in a skillet until translucent. Add the brown sugar and stir until the onion is coated. Cook until the onion is caramelized to a deep golden brown, stirring frequently.

Stir in the tomatoes, Alfredo sauce and artichokes. Season with the Greek seasoning and pepper. Cook until heated through, stirring occasionally. Divide hot cooked rice among dinner plates or shallow bowls. Spoon the chicken mixture over the top. Serve immediately.

Serves 4 to 6

Chicken with Forty Cloves of Garlic

40 garlic cloves (about 3 heads of garlic)
2 (3 1/2-pound) chickens
Kosher salt and freshly ground pepper to taste
1 tablespoon unsalted butter
2 tablespoons olive oil
2 tablespoons Cognac
1 1/2 cups dry white wine
1 tablespoon fresh thyme leaves
2 tablespoons all-purpose flour
1 tablespoon Cognac
2 tablespoons heavy cream

Separate the cloves of garlic. Blanch the garlic in enough boiling water to cover in a saucepan for 60 seconds. Drain and peel the garlic; set aside. Cut the chicken into pieces (four legs, four thighs and four breasts). Discard the remaining bones and wings. Cut the breasts into halves on the diagonal. Dry the chicken with paper towels and season liberally on both sides with salt and pepper.

Heat the butter and olive oil in a large heavy saucepan over medium-high heat. Add the chicken in batches, cooking each batch for 6 to 10 minutes or until golden brown. Turn each piece once with tongs or a spatula, being careful not to pierce the skin. If the butter and oil begin to burn, reduce the heat to medium. Remove the chicken to a plate, reserving the drippings in the saucepan.

Sauté the garlic in the reserved drippings over low heat for 5 to 10 minutes or until golden brown. Add 2 tablespoons Cognac and the wine. Simmer until thickened, stirring constantly and scraping up any brown bits from the bottom of the saucepan. Return the chicken and pan juices to the saucepan. Sprinkle with the thyme. Simmer, covered, over very low heat for 30 minutes or until the chicken is cooked through. Remove the chicken to a platter, reserving the sauce in the saucepan. Cover the chicken with foil and keep warm.

Whisk the flour and 1/2 cup of the reserved sauce in a small bowl. Whisk into the remaining sauce in the saucepan. Stir in 1 tablespoon Cognac and the cream and bring to a boil. Boil for 3 minutes, stirring frequently. Season with salt and pepper. Spoon the sauce over the chicken and serve immediately.

Serves 8

Asian Grilled Chicken with Spicy Noodles

Chicken
3 tablespoons soy sauce
2 teaspoons freshly grated ginger
2 garlic cloves, minced
4 chicken breasts
12 ounces spaghetti or angel hair pasta
1 red bell pepper, cut into strips
1 cup snow pea pods
5 green onions, sliced

Asian Dressing
2 tablespoons light brown sugar
2 tablespoons chili garlic sauce
2 1/2 tablespoons rice vinegar
2 1/2 tablespoons soy sauce
2 tablespoons vegetable oil
2 tablespoons sesame oil
2 tablespoons sesame seeds, toasted

For the chicken, mix the soy sauce, ginger and garlic in a sealable plastic bag. Add the chicken. Seal tightly and turn to coat. Chill for 4 hours, turning occasionally. Drain, discarding the marinade. Place the chicken on a grill rack and grill until cooked through. Let stand to cool. Slice into thin strips.

Cook the pasta according to the package directions. Rinse with cold water and drain. Combine the chicken, pasta, bell pepper, snow pea pods and green onions in a serving bowl. Toss to mix.

For the dressing, whisk the brown sugar, chili garlic sauce, vinegar and soy sauce in a bowl until combined. Add the vegetable oil and sesame oil gradually, whisking constantly until smooth. Drizzle over the chicken mixture. Sprinkle with the sesame seeds.

Serves 6

Commander's Chicken

4 to 6 chicken breasts
1/2 teaspoon salt
1/4 teaspoon pepper
1/2 cup all-purpose flour
1/4 cup corn oil
1 onion, chopped
1 green bell pepper, chopped
1/2 cup chopped celery
1 garlic clove, minced
1 teaspoon curry powder
1/4 teaspoon dried thyme
1 teaspoon salt
1/4 teaspoon pepper
2 (16-ounce) cans diced tomatoes
3 cups hot cooked rice

Pound the chicken between sheets of waxed paper with a meat mallet until flattened. Season with 1/2 teaspoon salt and 1/4 teaspoon pepper. Dredge in the flour, shaking off any excess. Brown the chicken in the hot corn oil in a skillet, turning occasionally. Remove the chicken to a plate and keep warm, reserving the drippings in the skillet.

Sauté the onion, bell pepper, celery and garlic in the reserved drippings until tender. Stir in the curry powder, thyme, 1 teaspoon salt and 1/4 teaspoon pepper. Stir in the tomatoes and bring to a boil. Return the chicken to the skillet. Reduce the heat and simmer, covered, for 30 minutes or until the chicken is cooked through and tender. Serve over the hot cooked rice.

Serves 4

Chicken Romano

1/3 cup all-purpose flour
1/2 teaspoon salt
1/4 teaspoon pepper
6 boneless skinless chicken breasts
2 tablespoons vegetable oil
1/4 cup minced onion
2 cups tomato juice
1 (4-ounce) jar sliced mushrooms, drained
2 tablespoons grated Romano cheese
1 tablespoon minced parsley
1 tablespoon sugar
1 teaspoon vinegar
1/2 teaspoon salt
1/2 teaspoon garlic salt
1/2 teaspoon oregano
1/4 teaspoon dried basil
16 ounces spaghetti
1/2 cup (2 ounces) grated Romano cheese

Mix the flour, 1/2 teaspoon salt and the pepper in a shallow dish. Dredge the chicken in the seasoned flour, shaking off any excess. Brown in the hot oil in a skillet. Remove to paper towels to drain, reserving 1 tablespoon of the drippings in the skillet. Sauté the onion in the reserved drippings until tender. Stir in the tomato juice, mushrooms, 2 tablespoons cheese, the parsley, sugar, vinegar, 1/2 teaspoon salt, the garlic salt, oregano and basil. Return the chicken to the skillet. Simmer, covered, for 45 minutes or until the chicken is cooked through and tender.

Cook the spaghetti according to the package directions; drain. Remove the spaghetti to a serving bowl or serving platter. Spoon the chicken mixture over the hot cooked pasta and sprinkle with 1/2 cup cheese.

Serves 6

Prosciutto and Asiago Chicken

6 boneless skinless chicken breasts
Salt and freshly ground pepper to taste
1 1/2 cups all-purpose flour
5 tablespoons butter
3/4 cup (3 ounces) finely grated asiago cheese
12 thin slices prosciutto
3 tablespoons butter
1/2 cup white wine
1/2 cup chopped green onions or shallots
1 tablespoon chopped fresh sage

Season the chicken with salt and pepper. Dredge in the flour, shaking off any excess. Brown in 5 tablespoons butter in a skillet over medium-high heat, turning once. Remove to a baking sheet. Sprinkle with the cheese. Top each piece of chicken with two slices of the prosciutto, pleated to fit to lie on top. Bake at 375 degrees for 5 minutes or until the chicken is cooked through. Remove to a serving platter. Reheat the skillet. Add 3 tablespoons butter, the wine, green onions and sage. Boil for 5 minutes or until reduced to 1/2 cup, stirring constantly and scraping up any brown bits from the bottom of the skillet. Spoon over the hot chicken. Serve immediately.

Serves 6

Stuffed Hickory Chicken

6 boneless skinless chicken breasts
1 (12-ounce) package stuffing mix
6 slices thick-cut hickory-smoked bacon
1 (10-ounce) can cream of mushroom soup
1 soup can milk
1 cup sour cream
Chopped fresh parsley

Pound the chicken between two sheets of waxed paper with a meat mallet until flattened. Prepare the stuffing mix according to the package directions. Spoon 1/4 to 1/3 cup stuffing onto each piece of chicken. Roll the chicken to enclose the stuffing. Wrap each piece of chicken with a slice of bacon and secure the end of the bacon with a wooden pick. Arrange in a baking dish. Bake at 350 degrees for 30 to 35 minutes or until the bacon begins to brown. Maintain the oven temperature.

Combine the soup, milk and sour cream in a saucepan. Bring almost to a boil, stirring frequently. Pour over the chicken. Bake until the internal temperature of the chicken reaches 165 degrees on a meat thermometer. Remove the wooden picks and slice the chicken. Arrange the slices in a shallow serving bowl and spoon the sauce over the top. Sprinkle with chopped parsley. The chicken may be stuffed and rolled 1 day in advance; chill, covered, until baking time.

For a variation, omit the bacon. Dip the rolled stuffed chicken in beaten egg. Roll in bread crumbs. Brown in olive oil in a skillet. Remove to a baking dish and continue to bake as directed.

For Spinach-Stuffed Chicken, fill the chicken with cooked drained spinach, rice pilaf and sliced Swiss cheese or sliced provolone cheese. For Chicken Cordon Bleu, fill the chicken with sliced or chopped ham and sliced cheese.

Serves 6

Tuscan Chicken Piccata

1/2 cup chopped shallots
1 rib celery, finely chopped
3 garlic cloves, minced
3 tablespoons olive oil
3/4 cup dry white wine
1 (28-ounce) can diced tomatoes with garlic, basil and oregano
1 teaspoon Cavender's Greek seasoning
1/4 cup capers, drained
1/4 teaspoon crushed red pepper flakes
6 boneless skinless chicken breasts
Salt and black pepper to taste
1/2 cup all-purpose flour
Pinch of cayenne pepper
3 eggs, lightly beaten
3/4 cup (3 ounces) grated Parmesan cheese
4 fresh basil leaves, thinly sliced
1/4 cup (1/2 stick) butter
2 tablespoons olive oil
Hot cooked risotto or hot cooked rice

Sauté the shallots, celery and garlic in 3 tablespoons olive oil in a skillet until translucent. Add the wine and cook for 3 minutes or until the wine is reduced by one-half. Stir in the tomatoes, Greek seasoning and capers. Simmer for 10 minutes. Stir in the red pepper flakes. Keep warm.

Pound the chicken breasts between two sheets of waxed paper if they are very thick. Season the chicken with salt and black pepper. Mix the flour and cayenne pepper on a plate. Mix the eggs, cheese and basil in a shallow bowl. Dredge the chicken in the flour, shaking off any excess. Dip immediately into the egg mixture. Cook the chicken in batches in the butter and 2 tablespoons olive oil in a hot skillet for 6 minutes or until brown, turning once. Remove the batches to a baking sheet and keep warm in the oven until serving time. Serve over hot cooked risotto. Spoon the hot tomato sauce over the top.

Serves 6

When browning meat, blot any moisture off the meat's surface with paper towels before cooking.

Chinese Pork and Rice

1 (3- to 4-pound) Boston butt pork roast
Browning and seasoning sauce to taste
Salt and pepper to taste
2/3 cup uncooked converted long grain rice
2 tablespoons vegetable oil
1 1/2 cups boiling water
1 teaspoon salt
1 beef bouillon cube
1 tablespoon soy sauce
1 onion, chopped
2 ribs celery, chopped
1 green bell pepper, chopped

Place the pork in a deep roasting pan. Drizzle with browning and seasoning sauce. Season with salt and pepper. Bake at 325 degrees for 5 to 6 hours. Chill until cool. Cut the pork into cubes. Brown the rice in the hot oil in a wok or deep skillet. Stir in the boiling water, 1 teaspoon salt, the bouillon cube and soy sauce. Cook, covered, for 20 minutes. Add the onion, celery, bell pepper and pork and mix well. Cook, covered, for 10 minutes longer.

Serves 4 to 6

Sweet Hot Barbecue Pork

1 (5- to 6-pound) Boston butt pork roast
1 cup sugar
1 teaspoon crushed red pepper flakes
1 teaspoon salt
1 1/2 cups vinegar
1/2 cup water

Place the pork fat side down in a deep roasting pan. Bake, covered, at 225 degrees for 6 to 8 hours or until the pork begins to fall apart. Shred into small pieces, discarding any fat and bone. Place in a 9×13-inch baking dish. Mix the sugar, red pepper flakes and salt in a bowl. Sprinkle over the pork. Mix the vinegar and water in a bowl. Pour over the pork. Bake, uncovered, for 1 to 2 hours longer or until the vinegar mixture is absorbed and the pork is brown, stirring every 20 to 30 minutes.

Serves 12

Honey Sesame Pork Tenderloin

1 cup chicken stock
$1/2$ cup soy sauce
3 tablespoons brown sugar
1 onion, chopped
2 garlic cloves, crushed
1 tablespoon sesame seeds
1 teaspoon ginger
$2^1/2$ to 3 pounds pork tenderloin
$1/2$ cup honey
$1/4$ cup sesame seeds
2 tablespoons cornstarch

Mix the stock, soy sauce, brown sugar, onion, garlic, 1 tablespoon sesame seeds and the ginger in a large sealable plastic bag. Add the pork. Seal tightly and turn to coat. Chill for 2 hours. Drain, reserving the marinade. Place the pork in a roasting pan sprayed with nonstick cooking spray. Brush with the honey, coating well. Sprinkle with $1/4$ cup sesame seeds. Bake at 350 degrees for 30 minutes or until cooked through. Bring the marinade to a boil in a saucepan. Stir in the cornstarch and cook until thickened. Slice the pork into medallions and serve with the sauce.

Serves 6

Sweet-and-Sour Pork Chops

4 bone-in pork chops
3 tablespoons vegetable oil
$1/2$ cup chopped onion
$1/3$ cup finely chopped celery
Juice of $1/2$ lemon
2 tablespoons brown sugar
1 teaspoon Dijon mustard
$1/2$ teaspoon salt
$1/4$ teaspoon pepper
1 (15-ounce) can tomato sauce
$1/2$ cup water

Brown the pork chops in the oil in a skillet. Remove to a 9×13-inch baking dish. Mix the onion, celery, lemon juice, brown sugar, Dijon mustard, salt and pepper in a bowl. Sprinkle over the pork chops. Mix the tomato sauce and water in a bowl. Pour over the pork chops. Bake, covered with foil, at 350 degrees for $1^1/4$ hours or until the pork chops are cooked through and tender.

Serves 4

Braised Zinfandel Brisket with Winter Root Vegetables

1 (4- to 5-pound) beef brisket, trimmed
3/4 teaspoon salt
1/4 teaspoon freshly ground black pepper
8 cups sliced sweet onions (about 4)
2 tablespoons sugar
1 teaspoon dried thyme
1/2 teaspoon salt
1/4 teaspoon freshly ground black pepper
2 carrots, cut into 1/2-inch slices
2 ribs celery, cut into 1/2-inch slices
6 garlic cloves, thinly sliced
2 cups red zinfandel or other fruity dry red wine
1/2 cup chicken broth
1/4 cup tomato paste
1 1/2 pounds small red potatoes, cut into quarters
3/4 teaspoon salt
1/4 teaspoon dried thyme
1 1/2 teaspoons extra-virgin olive oil
1 teaspoon dried oregano
1/4 teaspoon ground red pepper
Chopped fresh parsley to taste

Season the beef with 3/4 teaspoon salt and 1/4 teaspoon black pepper. Cook the beef in a large Dutch oven sprayed with nonstick cooking spray over medium-high heat for 8 minutes or until brown on all sides, turning once. Remove the beef to a platter, reserving the drippings in the Dutch oven. Cover and keep warm.

Cook the onions with the sugar, 1 teaspoon thyme, 1/2 teaspoon salt and 1/4 teaspoon black pepper in the reserved drippings until the onions are tender and golden brown, stirring occasionally. Add the carrots, celery and garlic. Cook for 5 minutes, stirring occasionally.

Place the beef on top of the vegetable mixture. Whisk together the wine, broth and tomato paste in a bowl. Pour over the beef. Bake, covered, at 325 degrees for 1 3/4 hours.

Combine the potatoes, 3/4 teaspoon salt, 1/4 teaspoon thyme, the olive oil, oregano and red pepper in a large bowl and toss to coat. Spread in a single layer on a baking sheet sprayed with nonstick cooking spray. Bake on the lower rack of the oven below the beef. Turn the beef and bake, covered, for 45 minutes longer or until the beef is tender.

Remove the beef from the oven and keep warm. Increase the oven temperature to 425 degrees. Bake the potatoes on the middle rack of the oven for 15 minutes or until the potatoes are crisp and the edges are brown. Slice the beef across the grain. Serve with the vegetable mixture and the potatoes. Sprinkle with parsley.

Serves 8

No-Fail Prime Rib

1 (4-rib) prime rib roast, bones trimmed and tied back onto the roast
Worcestershire sauce to taste
2 to 3 tablespoons minced garlic
1 cup sour cream
Prepared horseradish to taste

Place the beef in a roasting pan. Brush with Worcestershire sauce and rub with the garlic. Place in a cold oven. Set the oven temperature to 375 degrees and bake for 1 hour. Turn off the oven. Let the beef stand in the closed oven for 3 hours. Reset the oven emperature to 375 degrees and bake for 40 minutes. Remove from the oven and let stand for 10 minutes. Remove the bones and slice. Mix the sour cream and horseradish in a bowl. Serve with the beef.

Serves 8

Ask the butcher to cut the bones away from the roast and tie them back onto the roast. Once cooked, remove the bones. This makes the roast easier to carve without giving up the flavor.

Roasted Beef Tenderloin of "Van-der-vilt"

1 (3- to 4-pound) beef tenderloin, trimmed
Greek seasoning to taste
Salt to taste
Pepper to taste

Rub the beef with Greek seasoning, salt and pepper. Let stand for 30 minutes or until the beef reaches room temperature. Place on a rack in a baking pan or broiler pan. Add 1/2 inch of water to the baking pan; do not let the water touch the beef. Bake at 500 degrees to the desired degree of doneness. Bake for 5 minutes per pound for medium-rare or 7 minutes per pound for medium. Turn off the oven. Let the beef stand in the closed oven for 2 hours. Remove from the oven and let stand for 3 to 5 minutes before slicing.

Serves 8 to 10

Sarge at Large: *A trip to the Vanderbilts' (or as Sarge called them, the* Van-der-vilts'*) home, Biltmore Estate, gave us a lot of material, as you can tell!*

Savory Pepper Steak

1 (8-ounce) can tomatoes
1/4 cup all-purpose flour
1/2 teaspoon salt
1/8 teaspoon pepper
1 1/2 pounds sirloin steaks, cut into 1/2-inch strips
1/4 cup vegetable oil
1 3/4 cups water
1/2 cup chopped onion
1 garlic clove, minced
1 tablespoon beef-flavor gravy base
1 1/2 teaspoons Worcestershire sauce
2 large green bell peppers, cut into strips
1 to 2 tablespoons all-purpose flour (optional)
1 to 2 tablespoons cold water (optional)
Hot cooked rice

Drain the tomatoes, reserving the liquid. Mix the flour, salt and pepper together. Dredge the steak in the seasoned flour, shaking off any excess. Brown in the oil in a large skillet. Stir in the reserved liquid, water, onion, garlic and gravy base. Simmer, covered, for 1 1/4 hours or until the beef is tender. Stir in the Worcestershire sauce and bell peppers. Simmer, covered, for 5 minutes. If the sauce is too thin, mix equal parts flour and cold water in a bowl. Add gradually to the beef mixture, stirring constantly until thickened. Stir in the tomatoes and cook for 5 minutes. Serve over hot cooked rice.

Serves 6

Reuben "Kincaid" Casserole

1 3/4 cups sauerkraut, drained
8 ounces thinly sliced corned beef
2 cups (4 ounces) shredded Swiss cheese
3 tablespoons Thousand Island salad dressing
2 tomatoes, thinly sliced
1/2 cup (1 stick) butter
1 cup crushed rye crackers or crushed thin wheat crackers
1/4 cup caraway seeds (optional)

Layer the sauerkraut, corned beef, cheese, salad dressing and tomatoes in a 2-quart baking dish. Melt the butter in a saucepan. Add the crackers and caraway seeds and sauté briefly. Sprinkle over the tomatoes. Bake at 425 degrees for 30 minutes.

Serves 6 to 8

Sarge at Large: *This dish is named after Sarge's pet name for Madison Academy's resident PR man.*

Tuscan Lasagna

1 onion, finely chopped
1/2 carrot, finely chopped
1 rib celery, finely chopped
1 garlic clove, pressed
2 tablespoons fresh parsley, chopped
3 tablespoons olive oil
2 (28-ounce) cans tomatoes
2 pounds ground round
1/4 cup (1/2 stick) butter
4 cups milk
3 tablespoons cornstarch
1 teaspoon salt
1/2 teaspoon pepper
2 beef bouillon cubes
2 cups hot water
9 ounces no-cook lasagna noodles
2 1/2 cups (10 ounces) shredded Parmesan cheese

For the meat sauce, sauté the onion, carrot, celery, garlic and parsley in the olive oil in a large saucepan until the onion is translucent. Add the tomatoes and mix well. Add the ground round gradually, stirring constantly until brown. Simmer for 2 hours.

For the béchamel sauce, melt the butter in a saucepan. Mix the milk, cornstarch, salt and pepper in a bowl. Add to the butter gradually, stirring constantly. Cook until thickened, stirring constantly.

Dissolve the bouillon cubes in the hot water. Layer the pasta, bouillon, meat sauce, béchamel sauce and cheese one-third at a time in a 4-quart baking dish. Bake at 350 degrees for 1 hour. Pierce with a fork occasionally to check that the liquid is being absorbed into all of the pasta layers. Let stand for 10 minutes before slicing. This dish is great reheated and served the next day.

Serves 12

When assembling lasagna, alternate the direction of the layers of noodles. This helps the slices stay together better once served and keeps the filling from oozing.

A LA "CART"

No need to plug one of these dark green beauties grown on a Madison County farm in 1935 and brought to the public square for sale. The Huntsville–Madison County region has a mild climate, with an average growing season of about two hundred days a year, making it perfect for growing luscious fruits and vegetables year-round.

A la "Cart"

On the Side

Asparagus Bake

3 (8-ounce) cans asparagus spears, drained
3 tomatoes, peeled and thinly sliced
1/2 cup (1 stick) butter
1/2 cup mayonnaise
2 cups (8 ounces) shredded Cheddar cheese
1 teaspoon Worcestershire sauce
1/8 teaspoon Tabasco sauce, or to taste

Arrange the asparagus in two rows with the tips pointing outward and touching the long edges of a 9×13-inch baking dish. Arrange the tomatoes over the asparagus stems, leaving the tips exposed. Dot each tomato with some of the butter. Mix the mayonnaise, cheese, Worcestershire sauce and Tabasco sauce in a bowl. Mound over the tomatoes, leaving the asparagus tips exposed. Bake at 350 degrees for 20 minutes.

Serves 8

Baked Asparagus and Peas

1/4 cup (1/2 stick) butter
1/4 cup all-purpose flour
2 cups milk
1 (5-ounce) jar Old English cheese spread
10 saltine crackers, crushed
1 (15-ounce) can cut asparagus, drained
1 (15-ounce) can green peas, drained
1 (2-ounce) package sliced almonds
1 cup crushed cornflakes
Butter

Melt 1/4 cup butter in a saucepan. Stir in the flour. Cook for 1 minute, stirring constantly. Add the milk and cook over medium heat until thickened, stirring constantly. Add the cheese spread and cook until the cheese is melted, stirring constantly. Remove from the heat. Layer the crackers, asparagus, peas, almonds and cheese sauce one-half at a time in a 2-quart baking dish. Sprinkle with the cornflakes and dot with additional butter. Bake at 350 degrees for 30 minutes or until bubbly.

Serves 10 to 12

Petite Peas Casserole

1 cup chopped celery
1 cup chopped red bell pepper
1 cup chopped onion
1/2 cup (1 stick) butter
2 (15-ounce) cans tiny green peas, drained
1 (8-ounce) can water chestnuts, drained and chopped (optional)
1 (4-ounce) can chopped pimentos, drained
1 (10-ounce) can cream of mushroom soup
1 teaspoon white pepper
Salt to taste
1 (6-ounce) package herb-seasoned stuffing mix
1/4 cup (1/2 stick) butter, melted

Sauté the celery, bell pepper and onion in 1/2 cup butter in a skillet until tender. Stir in the peas, water chestnuts, pimentos, soup and 1 teaspoon white pepper. Season with salt and additional white pepper. Pour into a 9×13-inch baking dish. Cover with the stuffing mix. Drizzle with 1/4 cup melted butter. Bake at 350 degrees for 30 minutes.

Serves 10 to 12

Party Green Beans

1 (28-ounce) package frozen whole green beans
2 chicken bouillon cubes
1 (6-ounce) package sweetened dried cranberries, or to taste
4 ounces blue cheese, crumbled, or to taste
1 cup walnuts, toasted and coarsely chopped, or to taste

Boil the green beans with the bouillon cubes in enough water to cover in a large saucepan until tender; drain. Place the green beans in a decorative serving bowl. Top with the cranberries, blue cheese and walnuts. Serve immediately.

Serves 6 to 8

Sweet-and-Sour Green Beans

1 (16-ounce) package frozen
Italian green beans
Salt and pepper to taste
4 slices bacon
1 onion, chopped
1/3 cup sugar
1/2 cup vinegar

Prepare the green beans according to the package directions; drain. Season with salt and pepper. Cook the bacon in a large saucepan until crisp. Remove the bacon to paper towels to drain, reserving the drippings in the saucepan. Crumble the bacon. Sauté the onion in the reserved drippings until tender. Add the sugar and vinegar and cook until the sugar is dissolved and the mixture is thickened, stirring constantly. Add the green beans and toss to coat. Simmer for 10 minutes. Sprinkle with the bacon.

Serves 8

"Woof-gain-Pup's" Almond Broccoli Puff

1 pound broccoli
1/3 cup slivered almonds, toasted
2 tablespoons butter, melted
2 egg whites
1/2 cup mayonnaise
1/3 cup freshly grated Parmesan cheese
1 tablespoon grated onion

Steam the broccoli just until tender; drain. Arrange in a 9×13-inch baking dish with the stalks pointed toward the center of the baking dish. Sprinkle the stalks with the almonds and drizzle with the butter. Beat the egg whites in a mixing bowl until stiff peaks form. Fold in the mayonnaise, cheese and onion. Spread over the stalks of the broccoli. Bake for 5 minutes or until the center is puffed and brown.

Serves 8

Sarge at Large: *On a trip to New York, the group was talking about famous chefs. When Wolfgang Puck was mentioned, we knew that he would be a challenge, but she forged ahead with* "Woof-gain-Pup." *After trying countless times, crying with laughter, Sarge finally got it. Life is much sweeter with laughter.*

Roasted Broccoli with Sesame Dressing

2 pounds broccoli, trimmed to 3-inch stems
6 tablespoons olive oil
2 1/2 tablespoons fresh lemon juice
2 1/2 tablespoons soy sauce
2 tablespoons freshly chopped ginger
1 teaspoon minced garlic
1/2 teaspoon sugar
6 tablespoons vegetable oil
1 1/4 tablespoons sesame oil
1/4 cup toasted sesame seeds

Toss the broccoli with the olive oil on a baking sheet until coated. Bake at 500 degrees for 10 to 12 minutes, turning occasionally. Remove to a serving bowl. Process the lemon juice, soy sauce, ginger, garlic and sugar in a blender until combined. Add the vegetable oil and sesame oil in a fine stream, processing constantly until smooth. Pour over the broccoli. Sprinkle with the sesame seeds.

Serves 6 to 8

Maple-Glazed Carrots

2 pounds baby carrots
1/4 cup light Catalina salad dressing
1/4 cup maple syrup
1 tablespoon butter
1/2 cup pecan pieces, toasted

Boil the carrots in enough water to cover in a saucepan until tender; drain. Mix the salad dressing and maple syrup in a large saucepan. Cook over medium heat until bubbly. Add the carrots and toss to coat. Cook until the glaze is thickened, tossing occasionally. Add the butter and pecans. Cook until the butter is melted, stirring constantly.

Serves 8

Cheesy Dijon Cauliflower

Florets of 1 head cauliflower
1 cup mayonnaise
1 cup (4 ounces) shredded sharp Cheddar cheese
1 tablespoon Dijon mustard
1/4 onion, chopped
1 tablespoon parsley

Boil the cauliflower in enough water to cover in a saucepan just until tender; drain. Arrange in a 1 1/2-quart baking dish. Mix the mayonnaise, cheese, Dijon mustard, onion and parsley in a bowl. Spread over the cauliflower. Bake at 350 degrees until the cheese is melted.

Serves 6

Corn Pudding

1 (8-ounce) package corn muffin mix
1 (15-ounce) can cream-style corn
1 (15-ounce) can whole kernel corn, drained
1 (4-ounce) can diced green chiles,
drained (optional)
1 cup sour cream
1/2 cup (1 stick) butter, melted
1/4 cup chopped green onions (optional)
1 teaspoon freshly ground pepper
1 cup (4 ounces) shredded sharp Cheddar cheese

Mix the muffin mix, cream-style corn, whole kernel corn, green chiles, sour cream, butter, green onions and pepper in a bowl. Pour into an 8×8-inch baking dish. Bake at 350 degrees for 45 minutes or until golden brown. Sprinkle with the cheese and bake for 5 to 10 minutes longer or until the cheese is melted.

Serves 6 to 8

Twice-Baked Potatoes

8 baking potatoes
8 ounces cream cheese, softened
2 cups sour cream
1/2 cup (1 stick) butter, softened
8 slices bacon, crisp-cooked and crumbled
1/2 cup chopped green onions
2 garlic cloves, finely chopped
2 teaspoons seasoned salt
2 teaspoons seasoned pepper
1 teaspoon Cavender's Greek seasoning
2 cups (8 ounces) shredded Cheddar cheese

Bake the potatoes at 400 degrees for 1 hour or until soft. Let the potatoes stand to cool slightly. Cut into halves and scoop the pulp into a bowl, leaving the shells intact. Add the cream cheese, sour cream, butter, bacon, green onions, garlic, seasoned salt, seasoned pepper, Greek seasoning and 1 cup of the Cheddar cheese to the potato pulp and mix well. Spoon into the potato shells and place in a greased 9×13-inch baking dish. Bake at 350 degrees for 30 to 35 minutes. Sprinkle with the remaining 1 cup cheese and bake for 5 minutes longer or until the cheese is melted.

Serves 16

Cheesy New Potatoes

5 pounds new potatoes, cut into halves
2 bunches green onions, chopped
2 garlic cloves, chopped
2 tablespoons olive oil
2 cups sour cream
1 (10-ounce) can cream of mushroom soup
1 (10-ounce) can cream of chicken soup
1/4 cup (1/2 stick) butter
8 ounces bacon, crisp-cooked and crumbled
8 ounces sharp Cheddar cheese, shredded

Combine the potatoes and enough water to cover in a large saucepan or stockpot. Bring to a boil and boil until fork-tender; drain. Chop the potatoes into bite-size pieces and place in a bowl. Sauté the green onions and garlic in the olive oil in a skillet until tender. Add to the potatoes.

Mix the sour cream, mushroom soup, chicken soup, butter, bacon and 4 ounces of the cheese in a bowl. Fold into the potato mixture. Spoon into a greased 9×13-inch baking dish. Bake at 350 degrees for 30 minutes. Sprinkle with the remaining 4 ounces cheese and bake for 5 minutes longer or until the cheese is melted.

Serves 10 to 12

Yukon Gold and Sweet Potato Gratin

2 1/4 pounds Yukon Gold potatoes, peeled and thinly sliced
1 1/2 pounds red skinned sweet potatoes, peeled and thinly sliced
2 tablespoons butter, softened
2 cups milk
1 garlic clove, pressed
2 teaspoons fresh thyme leaves
1 tablespoon kosher salt
1 teaspoon pepper
1/8 teaspoon ground nutmeg
2 tablespoons butter, softened
1 cup whipping cream
2 tablespoons butter, softened

Arrange the potatoes and sweet potatoes in a 9×13-inch glass baking dish greased with 2 tablespoons butter. Mix the milk, garlic, thyme, salt, pepper and nutmeg in a saucepan. Bring to a boil, stirring frequently. Pour over the potatoes. Dot with 2 tablespoons butter. Bake, covered with foil, at 400 degrees for 50 minutes or until the potatoes are tender and most of the liquid has been absorbed. Bring the cream to a boil in a saucepan. Pour over the potatoes. Dot with 2 tablespoons butter. Bake, uncovered, for 25 minutes or until the top is golden brown. Let stand to cool slightly before serving.

Serves 12

Crisp Sweet Potato Fries

2 pounds sweet potatoes
1 tablespoon olive oil
1/4 teaspoon salt
1/4 teaspoon freshly ground pepper

Cut the potatoes into halves and then into 1/2-inch wedges. Combine with the olive oil, salt and pepper in a bowl and toss to coat. Arrange in a single layer on a foil-lined baking sheet sprayed with nonstick cooking spray. Bake at 450 degrees for 40 minutes or until brown and crisp, turning once. These are also great served as an appetizer.

Serves 4

Double-Baked Sweet Potatoes

6 sweet potatoes
4 ounces light cream cheese, softened
2 tablespoons butter, softened
1/3 cup packed light brown sugar
1/3 cup chopped pecans, toasted
1 tablespoon vanilla extract
1/4 teaspoon nutmeg
1/2 teaspoon pumpkin pie spice
1/2 teaspoon sea salt
1/2 teaspoon freshly ground pepper
48 pecan halves or miniature marshmallows

Pierce the sweet potatoes three or four times with a fork and place on a baking sheet. Bake at 350 degrees for 1 hour or just until tender. Let stand for 15 to 20 minutes. Cut each sweet potato lengthwise into halves with a serrated knife. Scoop the pulp into a bowl, leaving 1/3- to 1/2-inch shells. Place the shells in a large baking dish. Mash the sweet potato pulp in a large bowl. Mix the cream cheese, butter, brown sugar, 1/3 cup chopped pecans, the vanilla, nutmeg, pumpkin pie spice, salt and pepper in a bowl. Add to the sweet potato pulp and mix well. Spoon into the shells. Arrange four pecan halves on each sweet potato half. Bake at 350 degrees for 5 to 10 minutes or until heated through. These may be prepared 1 day in advance. Chill, covered, until baking time. Bake at 350 degrees for 20 to 25 minutes or until heated through.

Serves 12

Greek Feta Spinach

4 cups milk
1/2 cup (1 stick) butter
1/2 cup all-purpose flour
1/2 teaspoon white pepper
1/4 teaspoon salt, or to taste
2 pounds spinach
4 scallions, chopped
1/2 cup (1 stick) butter, melted
1/3 cup uncooked rice, rinsed and drained
8 ounces feta cheese, crumbled

Bring the milk almost to a boil in a large saucepan. Melt 1/2 cup butter in a small saucepan. Add the flour and stir until smooth. Add to the milk and simmer until thickened, stirring constantly. Remove from the heat and stir in the pepper and salt.

Steam the spinach and scallions until tender; drain. Pour 1/2 cup melted butter into a 9×13-inch baking dish and swirl the butter around, coating the bottom and sides of the dish evenly. Pour off any excess into a small bowl and reserve. Press the spinach mixture over the bottom of the dish. Layer the rice, cheese and sauce over the spinach. Drizzle with the reserved melted butter. Bake at 325 degrees for 45 minutes or until the top is firm.

Serves 6 to 8

Madison Academy Squash Dressing

2 cups cooked yellow squash
2 cups crumbled corn bread
1 onion, chopped
1 (10-ounce) can cream of celery soup or
cream of chicken soup
1/2 cup (1 stick) butter, melted
2 eggs, beaten
1 teaspoon sage

Mix the squash, corn bread, onion, soup, butter, eggs and sage in a bowl. Spoon into a greased 9×12-inch baking dish. Bake at 350 degrees for 30 minutes.

Serves 8 to 10

Roasted Root Vegetables

1 red onion, cut into wedges
4 carrots, sliced on the diagonal
1 turnip, peeled and cut into 1 1/2-inch pieces
1 rutabaga, peeled and cut into 1 1/2-inch pieces
1 large sweet potato, peeled and cut into 1 1/2-inch pieces
8 ounces brussels sprouts, cut into halves
1/2 cup extra-virgin olive oil
1 tablespoon dried oregano
1 tablespoon thyme
1 tablespoon rosemary
1 tablespoon dried basil
1 tablespoon kosher salt
1/4 teaspoon freshly ground pepper

Combine the onion, carrots, turnip, rutabaga, sweet potato and brussels sprouts in a bowl. Add the olive oil, oregano, thyme, rosemary, basil, salt and pepper. Toss until all of the vegetables are coated with the olive oil and herbs. Spread on a large heavy baking sheet. Bake at 400 degrees for 35 to 45 minutes or until tender and golden brown, stirring occasionally.

Serves 8 to 10

Vegetable Caponata

1 rib celery, chopped
1 red onion, chopped
1 red bell pepper, cut into 1/2-inch pieces
1/4 cup olive oil
1 eggplant, cut into 1/2-inch pieces
1 (14-ounce) can diced tomatoes
3 tablespoons golden raisins
1/2 teaspoon dried oregano
1/4 cup red wine vinegar
1 tablespoon drained capers
1 teaspoon sugar
1/2 teaspoon salt
1 teaspoon freshly ground pepper

Sauté the celery, onion and bell pepper in the hot olive oil in a skillet for 3 minutes or until tender. Add the eggplant and sauté for 2 minutes or until the eggplant is softened. Add the undrained tomatoes, raisins and oregano. Simmer over low heat for 20 minutes, stirring frequently. Stir in the vinegar, capers, sugar, salt and pepper.

Serves 6 to 8

Curried "Fru-ta-tion" Bake

1/3 cup butter, melted
1 cup packed brown sugar
1 tablespoon curry powder
Pinch of cinnamon
1 (30-ounce) can pears, drained
1 (30-ounce) can apricot halves, drained, or
  sliced peaches, drained
1 (20-ounce) can pineapple chunks, drained
1 (10-ounce) jar maraschino cherries, drained

Mix the butter, brown sugar, curry powder and cinnamon in a bowl. Add the pears, apricots, pineapple and cherries. Toss to coat. Pour into a 2-quart baking dish and bake at 325 degrees for 35 minutes.

Serves 8 to 10

Sarge at Large: *Congratulating a first-year teacher on a successful year, Sarge patted him on the back and said, "See there, I told you everything would come to* fru-ta-tion *(fruition)!" Sarge is always the encourager.*

Out-of-This-World Macaroni and Cheese

1 cup (4 ounces) shredded sharp Cheddar cheese
1 cup (4 ounces) shredded Gruyère cheese
1 cup (4 ounces) shredded Swiss cheese
1 1/2 cups chopped Brie cheese, rind trimmed
16 ounces large elbow macaroni
1/4 cup (1/2 stick) butter
1/4 cup all-purpose flour
2 teaspoons fresh thyme, chopped
1 teaspoon nutmeg
3 cups fat-free half-and-half
1 cup heavy cream
2 cups fresh bread crumbs, buttered and toasted
1 tablespoon butter

Mix the Cheddar cheese, Gruyère cheese, Swiss cheese and Brie cheese in a bowl. Remove 1/2 cup of the cheese mixture and reserve. Cook the pasta according to the package directions until al dente; drain.

Melt 1/4 cup butter in a large saucepan over medium heat. Add the flour and cook for 4 minutes or until the mixture is brown, stirring constantly. Stir in the thyme and nutmeg. Add the half-and-half and cream gradually, stirring constantly. Simmer until thickened, stirring constantly. Add the remaining cheese mixture and cook until the cheese is melted, stirring constantly. Remove from the heat and fold in the pasta.

Pour into a 9×13-inch baking dish. Sprinkle with the reserved cheese mixture and the bread crumbs. Dot with 1 tablespoon butter. Bake at 375 degrees for 20 minutes or until bubbly.

Serves 8

Pasta and Rice Bake

1 cup (2 sticks) butter
8 ounces uncooked thin spaghetti or angel hair pasta
2 cups uncooked converted white rice
2 (10-ounce) cans French onion soup
2 (10-ounce) cans chicken broth
2 (10-ounce) cans beef broth

Melt the butter in a large saucepan. Add the pasta and cook until honey-colored, tossing constantly. Fold in the rice. Stir in the soup, chicken broth and beef broth. Cook for 15 to 30 minutes or until most of the liquid has been absorbed. Spoon into a greased 9×13-inch baking dish. Bake, covered, at 350 degrees for 15 minutes. Bake, uncovered, for 15 minutes longer.

Serves 15 to 18

Basmati Rice

2 cups water
2 tablespoons butter
1 cup basmati rice
2 teaspoons chicken bouillon granules
1 tablespoon minced onion, or 1/4 cup chopped green onions
1 to 2 teaspoons curry powder

Combine the water and butter in a saucepan. Bring to a boil. Stir in the rice, bouillon granules, onion and curry. Reduce the heat and simmer, covered, for 20 minutes. Jasmine rice may be substituted for the basmati rice.

Serves 4 to 6

Bachelor Brown Rice

1 cup rice
1/2 cup (1 stick) butter, melted
1 (10-ounce) can beef consommé
1 (10-ounce) can French onion soup
1/2 cup (2 ounces) freshly grated Parmesan cheese

Mix the rice, butter, consommé and soup in a 5-quart baking dish. Top with the cheese. Bake at 350 degrees for 1 hour.

Serves 4 to 6

Stir-Fried Chinese Rice

3 cups white rice
3 cups brown rice
1 cup wild rice
1 (8-ounce) can water chestnuts, drained and chopped
1 (8-ounce) can bamboo sprouts, drained and chopped
1 cup chopped mushrooms
1/2 cup chopped green onions
3/4 cup slivered almonds, toasted
1 (16-ounce) package frozen green peas and carrots
1/2 cup peanut oil or canola oil
1/2 cup soy sauce

Cook the white rice, brown rice and wild rice according to the package directions; drain. Combine the rices in a bowl. Add the water chestnuts, bamboo sprouts, mushrooms, green onions, almonds and peas and carrots and toss to mix. Heat the peanut oil and soy sauce in a large skillet. Add the rice mixture and cook until heated through, stirring constantly.

For a variation, add one 6-ounce package dried cranberries for an added zing.

Serves 6 to 8

Baked Cashew Rice

1/2 cup (1 stick) margarine
12 ounces mushrooms, sliced
6 green onions, sliced
2 garlic cloves, minced
2 cups brown rice
1/2 teaspoon dried thyme
1 teaspoon salt
1/2 teaspoon freshly ground pepper, or to taste
6 cups chicken broth
1 1/2 cups coarsely chopped cashews, toasted
1/4 cup chopped fresh parsley
1 handful whole cashews

Melt the margarine in a 5-quart Dutch oven over medium heat. Add the mushrooms, green onions and garlic. Sauté for 5 minutes or until tender. Add the rice and cook for 1 minute, stirring constantly. Add the thyme, salt and pepper and mix well. Stir in the broth and bring to a boil. Bake, covered, at 400 degrees for 1 1/2 hours or until the rice is tender and all the liquid has been absorbed. Stir in the chopped cashews. Spoon into a serving dish. Sprinkle with the parsley and the whole cashews.

Serves 20

Out of This World

Southern traditions are deeply rooted in our soil and our hearts. Our history and traditions define not only who we are, but who we may become. Cotton made the south a unique entity, and it made Huntsville a major center of commerce through its people and culture. Cotton is still farmed in Madison County; however, the changes from the 1860s to the 1960s dictated that row cropping give way to transistors and rocket boosters. The SA-9 developed at Redstone Arsenal was one of many technological miracles produced by the region, people, and culture who also gave us grits and corn bread. As we move into the future, we continue to hold on to these cherished traditions. Now, we readily await the inevitable changes to come. Let the countdown continue.

Out of This World

Sweet Endings

"Dewy" Apple Dumplings

4 Granny Smith apples
2 (8-count) cans refrigerator crescent rolls
1 cup (2 sticks) butter
1 1/3 cups sugar
1/2 teaspoon cinnamon
1 (12-ounce) can Mountain Dew

Peel and core the apples. Slice the apples into quarters. Unroll the dough. Roll each apple slice in a crescent roll and arrange in a 9×13-inch baking pan. Melt the butter in a saucepan. Stir in the cinnamon and sugar. Pour over the crescent rolls. Pour the Mountain Dew over the top. Bake at 350 degrees for 45 minutes. Serve warm with vanilla ice cream.

Serves 8

Bright Star Peach Cobbler

1/2 cup (1 stick) butter
1 cup sugar
1 cup orange juice
1 (8-count) can crescent rolls
1 (15-ounce) can peach halves, drained
1 teaspoon cinnamon
1 teaspoon sugar

Melt the butter in a cast-iron skillet. Stir in 1 cup sugar and the orange juice and bring to a simmer. Simmer for 5 to 10 minutes, stirring frequently. Unroll the dough. Roll a crescent roll around each peach half and place in the orange juice mixture in the skillet. Sprinkle with the cinnamon and 1 teaspoon sugar. Bake at 350 degrees for 15 minutes or until golden brown.

Serves 8

White Chocolate Crème Brûlée

8 egg yolks
6 tablespoons granulated sugar
3 cups heavy whipping cream
6 tablespoons granulated sugar
1 vanilla bean
6 ounces good-quality white
chocolate, chopped
1/2 teaspoon vanilla extract
1/2 cup packed brown sugar
1/2 cup confectioners' sugar
1/4 cup granulated sugar

Combine the egg yolks and 6 tablespoons granulated sugar in a bowl, stirring until the sugar is dissolved; set aside. Combine the cream and 6 tablespoons granulated sugar in a saucepan. Cut the vanilla bean into halves lengthwise. Scrape the vanilla seeds from the pod with the back of a knife. Stir the vanilla seeds into the cream mixture. Discard or reserve the vanilla pod for another use. Bring the cream mixture to a gentle boil, stirring frequently. Add the white chocolate and stir until the white chocolate is melted. Remove from the heat and stir in the vanilla.

Stir 1 cup of the hot cream mixture into the egg yolk mixture to temper; then stir the egg yolk mixture into the remaining cream mixture in the saucepan. Divide among twelve ovenproof ramekins. Arrange in a large deep baking pan. Add enough hot water to the larger pan to reach the custard line. Bake at 300 degrees for 40 minutes or until the centers are set. Remove the ramekins carefully from the water bath.

Mix the brown sugar, confectioners' sugar and 1/4 cup granulated sugar in a bowl. Sprinkle 1 to 2 teaspoons of the mixture over each custard. Brown the sugar mixture using a crème brûlée torch or place on a baking sheet and broil until the sugar mixture is golden brown.

Serves 12

White Chocolate Bread Pudding

1 loaf French bread
3 eggs
8 egg yolks
4 cups heavy cream
$1^1/_2$ cups milk
$^1/_2$ cup sugar
2 cups (12 ounces) white chocolate chips

Cut the bread into $^3/_4$-inch slices. Cut the slices into cubes and arrange on a baking sheet. Bake at 350 degrees for 15 minutes or until toasted, tossing once. Arrange the bread in a greased 9×13-inch baking dish.

Whisk the eggs and egg yolks in a bowl until combined. Combine the cream, milk and sugar in a saucepan. Bring to a boil over medium heat, stirring frequently. Remove from the heat and stir in the white chocolate. Stir until the white chocolate is melted and the mixture is smooth. Add to the eggs gradually, whisking constantly. Pour over the bread and press the bread into the cream. Chill, covered, for 1 hour. Bake at 300 degrees for 1 hour or until a knife inserted into the center comes out clean. Let stand for 15 minutes before serving.

Serves 10 to 15

Bread puddings are a great way to use up day-old or stale bread.

"Homeland Security" Banana Pudding

6 tablespoons (heaping) all-purpose flour
1 1/2 cups sugar
1 1/2 teaspoons salt
4 cups milk
2 cups half-and-half
11 medium egg yolks, lightly beaten
1 teaspoon vanilla extract
1 (12-ounce) package vanilla wafers
5 or 6 bananas, sliced
11 medium egg whites
1/4 teaspoon cream of tartar
6 to 8 tablespoons sugar

Mix the flour, 1 1/2 cups sugar and the salt together. Combine the milk and half-and-half in a saucepan. Heat over low heat until lukewarm. Add the flour mixture gradually, stirring constantly. Combine 1/2 cup of the milk mixture and 11 egg yolks in a bowl. Stir until smooth. Pour into the remaining milk mixture in the saucepan. Cook until thickened, stirring constantly. Remove from the heat and stir in the vanilla. Let stand until cool. Reserve six vanilla wafers. Arrange the remaining vanilla wafers in a 9×13-inch glass baking dish. Layer with the bananas and pudding. Stir gently to moisten. Crush the reserved vanilla wafers over the top of the pudding.

Beat the egg whites and cream of tartar in a mixing bowl until foamy. Add 6 to 8 tablespoons sugar gradually, beating constantly until stiff peaks form. Spread over the pudding, sealing to the edges. Bake at 350 degrees for 8 to 10 minutes or until the meringue is golden brown.

Serves 15

Sarge at Large: *After 9/11, security on our motor coach was very heightened, especially when traveling with Sarge! Every bag had to have a "Homeland Security" tag attached, and that became the "key phrase" of her trips. We thought those tags brought us security . . . just wait until you experience the comfort found in this banana pudding!*

Frozen Berries with White Chocolate Cream

20 ounces good-quality white chocolate, coarsely chopped
2 1/2 cups heavy cream
5 teaspoons vanilla extract
2 1/4 pounds frozen mixed berries or frozen raspberries

Combine the white chocolate, cream and vanilla in a heatproof bowl. Place over a saucepan of simmering water and simmer until the white chocolate is melted, stirring occasionally. Arrange the frozen berries in dessert bowls 5 minutes before serving time. Spoon the warm sauce over the berries and serve immediately.

Serves 8

Frosted Strawberry Squares

1 cup sifted all-purpose flour
1/2 cup chopped toasted pecans
1/4 cup packed brown sugar
1/2 cup (1 stick) butter, softened
1 cup heavy whipping cream
2 egg whites
1 cup granulated sugar
2 cups strawberries, chopped
1 tablespoon lemon juice

Mix the flour, pecans, brown sugar and butter in a bowl until crumbly. Spread on a rimmed baking sheet. Bake at 350 for 30 minutes, stirring frequently. Sprinkle two-thirds of the crumb mixture in a 9×13-inch glass baking dish. Beat the cream in a mixing bowl until firm peaks form; set aside. Combine the egg whites, granulated sugar, strawberries and lemon juice in a mixing bowl. Beat at high speed for 10 minutes. Fold in the whipped cream. Spoon over the crumb layer. Sprinkle with the remaining crumb mixture. Freeze, covered, for 6 to 10 hours. Slice and serve.

Serves 15

Cherry Berries on a Cloud

6 egg whites
1/2 teaspoon cream of tartar
1/4 teaspoon salt
1 3/4 cups sugar
6 ounces cream cheese, softened
1 cup sugar
1 teaspoon vanilla extract
1 cup sour cream
1 cup whipped topping
2 cups miniature marshmallows
1 (16-ounce) can cherry pie filling
16 ounces frozen sliced strawberries
2 cups fresh strawberries, sliced
1 teaspoon lemon juice

Beat the egg whites, cream of tartar and salt in a mixing bowl until foamy. Add 1 3/4 cups sugar and beat for 5 minutes or until stiff peaks form and the mixture is very glossy. Spread in a greased 9×13-inch baking pan. Bake at 275 degrees for 1 hour. Turn off the oven. Let the meringue stand in the closed oven until cool.

Beat the cream cheese, 1 cup sugar and the vanilla in a bowl until smooth. Fold in the sour cream, whipped topping and marshmallows. Spread over the meringue shell. Chill, covered, for 8 to 10 hours. Mix the pie filling, frozen strawberries, fresh strawberries and lemon juice in a bowl. Spoon over the cream cheese layer just before serving.

Serves 12

Royal Meringue Dessert

1 banana
Orange juice
2 navel oranges
1 cup egg whites (about 6), at room temperature
1/2 teaspoon cream of tartar
1/2 teaspoon salt
1 1/2 cups granulated sugar
2 cups heavy whipping cream
1/2 cup confectioners' sugar
3/4 cup drained pineapple chunks, chilled
3/4 cup seedless green grapes
1 ounce German's sweet chocolate, shaved

Slice the banana and dip in orange juice. Chill until needed. Peel and section the oranges. Chill until needed.

Beat the egg whites, cream of tartar and salt in a mixing bowl until soft peaks form. Add the granulated sugar 2 tablespoons at a time, beating constantly until shiny and stiff peaks form. Drop by tablespoonfuls onto two lightly buttered and floured baking sheets, using a rubber spatula to help release the meringue from the spoon; mound the meringue. Bake at 275 degrees for 1 hour or just until crisp and golden brown. Cool on a wire rack.

Beat the whipping cream and confectioners' sugar in a mixing bowl until firm peaks form. Drain the banana and orange, discarding any juice. Fold in three-fourths of the banana, three-fourths of the orange sections, three-fourths of the pineapple and three-fourths of the grapes. Arrange twelve meringues closely to form a 9-inch disc on a serving platter. Layer half of the cream mixture over the meringues, mounding the mixture. Continue to layer the meringues and the cream mixture, mounding in the shape of a cone and ending with the meringues. Fill the spaces between the meringues with the cream mixture and top with one meringue. Decorate with the remaining banana, orange, pineapple and grapes. Sprinkle with the shaved chocolate. Chill for 4 hours. Spoon onto dessert plates to serve.

You may also layer this dessert in a glass trifle dish or prepare in individual ramekins or dessert bowls.

Serves 12

Scrumptious Ritz Torte

Torte

3 egg whites
1/2 teaspoon baking powder
1 cup sugar
20 Ritz crackers, crushed
3/4 cup chopped pecans
1 teaspoon vanilla extract
Freshly whipped cream or
whipped topping

Chocolate Topping (optional)

1 (8-ounce) chocolate candy bar, chopped
1 tablespoon butter
4 ounces whipped topping or whipped cream

For the torte, beat the egg whites and baking powder in a mixing bowl until soft peaks form. Add the sugar 1 tablespoon at a time, beating constantly until stiff peaks form. Fold in the crackers, pecans and vanilla. Spoon into a greased 8×8-inch baking dish. Bake at 325 degrees for 30 minutes. Let stand until cool.

For the topping, combine the candy bar and butter in a microwave-safe bowl. Microwave on High at 20- to 30-second intervals until melted and smooth, stirring after each interval. Stir in the whipped topping. Spread over the cooled torte. Chill for 1 hour.

To serve, top with whipped cream. Garnish with chocolate curls, maraschino cherries and/or chopped or whole pecans. Cut into squares.

Serves 16

Pineapple Blitz Torte

1 cup cake flour
1/4 tablespoon baking powder
1/4 tablespoon salt
1/4 cup (1/2 stick) butter, softened
1/2 cup granulated sugar
4 egg yolks, lightly beaten
1/3 cup milk
4 egg whites
3/4 cup granulated sugar
1/4 teaspoon vanilla extract
3/4 cup chopped pecans, toasted
1 cup heavy whipping cream
1 1/2 tablespoons confectioners' sugar
1 cup drained crushed pineapple
1/4 teaspoon vanilla extract

Sift the cake flour, baking powder and salt together. Cream the butter and 1/2 cup granulated sugar in a mixing bowl until light and fluffy. Beat in the egg yolks. Add the sifted dry ingredients and milk alternately, mixing well after each addition. Pour into two greased and floured 8-inch cake pans. Bake at 350 degrees for 15 minutes. Maintain the oven temperature.

Beat the egg whites in a mixing bowl until soft peaks form. Add 3/4 cup granulated sugar 1 tablespoon at a time, beating constantly at high speed until stiff peaks form. Beat in 1/4 teaspoon vanilla. Spread over the partially baked cake layers. Sprinkle each with half the pecans. Bake for 15 minutes. The meringue will rise while cooking but will fall as it cools. Cool in the cake pans.

Beat the whipping cream in a bowl until firm peaks form. Fold in the confectioners' sugar, pineapple and 1/4 teaspoon vanilla. Invert one cake layer meringue side down onto a serving plate. Spread the whipped cream mixture over the top. Top with the remaining cake layer meringue side up.

Serves 12

Orchard Apple Cake with Buttermilk Glaze

Cake
3 cups sifted all-purpose flour
1 teaspoon baking soda
1 teaspoon cinnamon
1 teaspoon ground cloves
1/2 teaspoon salt
3 eggs
2 cups sugar
1 1/2 cups vegetable oil
1/2 cup orange juice
1 cup chopped pecans
1 cup shredded coconut
1 cup finely chopped
Granny Smith apple
1/2 cup golden raisins
All-purpose flour

Buttermilk Glaze
1 cup sugar
1/2 cup (1 stick) butter
1/2 cup buttermilk
1 tablespoon corn syrup
1/2 teaspoon baking soda
1 teaspoon vanilla extract

For the cake, sift 3 cups flour, the baking soda, cinnamon, cloves and salt together. Combine the eggs, sugar and oil in a mixing bowl. Beat until smooth. Add the orange juice and beat until smooth. Add the sifted dry ingredients and beat until smooth. Toss the pecans, coconut, apple and raisins in additional flour, discarding any excess flour. Stir into the batter. Pour into a greased and floured bundt pan. Bake at 325 degrees for 1 1/2 hours.

For the glaze, mix the sugar, butter, buttermilk, corn syrup and baking soda in a saucepan. Bring to a boil, stirring frequently. Remove from the heat and stir in the vanilla. Poke holes in the top of the cake. Pour the glaze over the cake and let stand for 1 hour. Invert onto a serving plate.

Two additional cups of chopped apples may be substituted for the raisins and coconut, if desired. This glaze is also great served over angel food cake.

Serves 12

Glazed Coconut Pound Cake

2 cups all-purpose flour
$1\frac{1}{2}$ teaspoons baking powder
1 teaspoon salt
1 cup shortening
2 cups sugar
5 eggs
1 cup buttermilk
$1\frac{1}{2}$ teaspoons coconut extract
1 (7-ounce) can sweetened flaked coconut
1 cup sugar
$\frac{1}{2}$ cup hot water
1 teaspoon coconut extract

Sift the flour, baking powder and salt together. Cream the shortening and 2 cups sugar in a mixing bowl until light and fluffy. Add the eggs one at a time, beating well after each addition. Add the sifted dry ingredients and buttermilk alternately, mixing well after each addition. Stir in $1\frac{1}{2}$ teaspoons coconut extract and the coconut. Pour into a greased tube pan. Bake at 350 degrees for 50 to 60 minutes or until a wooden pick inserted into the center of the cake comes out clean.

Combine 1 cup sugar and the water in a saucepan. Bring to a boil and boil for 2 minutes. Remove from the heat and stir in 1 teaspoon coconut extract. Invert the cake onto a serving plate. Poke holes in the top of the cake with a wooden pick and drizzle with the glaze.

Serves 16

Miss Francis's Chocolate Pound Cake with Fudge Frosting

Cake
3 cups sifted all-purpose flour
1/2 cup baking cocoa
1/2 teaspoon baking powder
1/4 teaspoon salt
1 cup (2 sticks) butter, softened
1/2 cup shortening
3 cups sugar
5 eggs
1 1/4 cups milk
1 teaspoon vanilla extract

Fudge Frosting
2 cups sugar
3 tablespoons baking cocoa
1/2 cup milk
1/4 cup light corn syrup
1/2 cup (1 stick) margarine

For the cake, mix the flour, baking cocoa, baking powder and salt together. Cream the butter, shortening and sugar in a mixing bowl until light and fluffy. Add the eggs one at a time, mixing well after each addition. Add the dry ingredients and milk alternately, mixing well after each addition. Beat in the vanilla. Pour into a greased and floured tube pan. Bake at 325 degrees for 1 hour. Cool in the pan. Invert onto a serving plate.

For the frosting, mix the sugar and baking cocoa in a bowl. Stir in the milk and corn syrup. Melt the margarine in a saucepan. Stir in the baking cocoa mixture and bring to a boil. Boil for 1 minute. Remove from the heat. Beat until the mixture is of a spreading consistency. Spread over the cooled cake immediately; spoon any excess frosting into the hole in the middle of the cake.

Serves 12

Italian Cream Cake

Cake

2 cups sifted all-purpose flour
1 teaspoon baking soda
1/2 cup (1 stick) butter, softened
1/2 cup shortening
2 cups sugar
5 egg yolks
1 cup buttermilk
1 teaspoon vanilla extract
1 (3-ounce) can sweetened flaked coconut
5 egg whites

Cream Cheese Pecan Frosting

1/2 cup (1 stick) butter, softened
8 ounces cream cheese, softened
1 (1-pound) package confectioners' sugar
1 tablespoon vanilla extract
1/2 cup toasted chopped pecans

For the cake, mix the flour and baking soda together. Cream the butter, shortening and sugar in a mixing bowl until light and fluffy. Add the egg yolks one at a time, mixing well after each addition. Add the dry ingredients and buttermilk alternately, mixing well after each addition and beginning and ending with the dry ingredients. Stir in the vanilla and coconut. Beat the egg whites in a mixing bowl until stiff peaks form. Fold into the batter. Pour into three greased and floured 9-inch cake pans. Bake at 300 degrees for 45 minutes. Cool in the pans.

For the frosting, cream the butter, cream cheese, confectioners' sugar and vanilla in a mixing bowl until light and fluffy. Stir in the pecans. Spread between the layers and over the top and side of the cake.

Serves 12 to 15

Cottontail's Carrot Cake

3 cups sifted all-purpose flour
1 tablespoon baking powder
2 teaspoons baking soda
1 1/2 teaspoons cinnamon
1/2 teaspoon salt
1 cup packed light brown sugar
1 cup granulated sugar
1 1/2 cups vegetable oil
4 eggs
2 cups grated carrots
1/2 cup pecans, chopped
1/2 cup dates, chopped
1/2 cup raisins
All-purpose flour
1/2 cup (1 stick) margarine, softened
8 ounces cream cheese, softened
1 (1-pound) package confectioners' sugar
1 teaspoon vanilla extract
1 cup toasted chopped pecans

Mix 3 cups flour, the baking powder, baking soda, cinnamon and salt together. Mix the brown sugar, granulated sugar and oil in a bowl. Add the eggs one at a time, mixing well after each addition. Stir in the dry ingredients. Toss the carrots, pecans, dates and raisins in flour to coat; discard any excess flour. Stir into the batter. Pour into three greased and floured 8-inch cake pans. Bake at 350 degrees for 1 hour. Cool in the pans.

Cream the margarine, cream cheese and confectioners' sugar in a mixing bowl until light and fluffy. Stir in the vanilla and pecans. Spread between the layers and over the top and side of the cake.

Serves 12 to 16

Smooth-as-Silk Chocolate Layer Cake

2 cups all-purpose flour
1 teaspoon baking soda
1/2 teaspoon salt
1 cup sour cream
2 teaspoons vanilla extract
1/2 cup (1 stick) butter, softened
1 (1-pound) package brown sugar
3 eggs
1 1/2 cups (9 ounces) semisweet chocolate chips, melted
1 cup hot water
Mother's Chocolate Frosting (page 27)
or Cream Cheese Pecan Frosting (page 136)

Sift the flour, baking soda and salt together. Mix the sour cream and vanilla in a small bowl. Cream the butter and brown sugar in a mixing bowl until light and fluffy. Add the eggs one at a time, mixing well after each addition. Add the chocolate and mix until smooth. Add the sifted dry ingredients and sour cream mixture alternately, mixing well after each addition. Add the water in a fine stream, mixing constantly. Pour into three greased and floured 8-inch cake pans. Bake at 350 degrees for 40 minutes or until a wooden pick inserted into the center of the layers comes out clean. Cool in the pans. Spread the frosting between the layers and over the top and side of the cake.

Serves 12 to 15

When making a chocolate cake from a packaged cake mix, substitute cold brewed coffee for the water. The coffee enhances the chocolate flavor, and the cake will taste like it was made from scratch.

French Christmas Cake

1 cup (2 sticks) butter, softened
2 cups sugar
6 eggs
1 (12-ounce) package vanilla wafers,
  finely crushed
1/2 cup milk
1 (7-ounce) can sweetened flaked coconut
11/2 cups chopped pecans

Cream the butter and sugar in a mixing bowl until light and fluffy. Add the eggs one at a time, mixing well after each addition. Add the vanilla wafers and milk alternately, mixing well after each addition. Stir in the coconut and pecans. Pour into a greased and floured tube pan or bundt pan. Bake at 350 degrees for 11/2 hours. Cool completely in the pan. Remove to a serving plate. The cake is delicate and will break if removed from the pan before it is completely cool.

Serves 12

Aunt Polly's Old-Fashioned Tea Cakes

5 cups all-purpose flour
1 teaspoon baking soda
1 teaspoon salt
1 cup shortening
1/2 cup (1 stick) margarine, softened
1/2 cup (1 stick) butter, softened
2 cups sugar
2 eggs
2 teaspoons vanilla extract
Sugar

Mix the flour, baking soda and salt together. Cream the shortening, margarine, butter and 2 cups sugar in a mixing bowl until light and fluffy. Add the eggs one at a time, mixing well after each addition. Add the dry ingredients and vanilla; mix well. Shape the dough into walnut-size balls. Roll in additional sugar. Arrange on a nonstick cookie sheet. Flatten with the bottom of a glass. Bake at 350 degrees for 8 to 10 minutes or just until the edges are golden brown.

Makes 6 dozen

Brown Butter Pecan Shortbread

$1/2$ cup (1 stick) salted butter, softened
1 cup toasted pecans
2 cups sifted all-purpose flour
$1/4$ teaspoon coarse kosher salt
$1/2$ cup (1 stick) salted butter, softened
$1/2$ cup sugar
1 teaspoon vanilla extract

Melt $1/2$ cup butter in a skillet. Cook for 5 to 6 minutes or until the butter turns dark amber, stirring frequently. Strain into a bowl. Chill for 1 hour or just until firm. Process the pecans in a food processor to the consistency of coarse meal. Mix the flour and salt together. Cream the brown butter, $1/2$ cup butter and the sugar in a mixing bowl until light and fluffy. Stir in the pecans and vanilla. Add the flour mixture gradually, mixing well after each addition.

Shape the dough into a rectangle on a sheet of baking parchment. Top with another sheet of baking parchment and roll the dough into an 8×12-inch rectangle. Remove the baking parchment and place the dough on a nonstick cookie sheet. Poke with a fork once every inch. Bake at 300 degrees for 55 minutes or until golden brown and firm. Slice lengthwise into eight strips. Slice each strip crosswise into eight pieces. Cool on the cookie sheet on a wire rack for 10 minutes. Remove to the wire rack to cool completely. These may be prepared up to 3 days in advance. Store in a covered container at room temperature.

Makes $3\frac{1}{2}$ dozen

Mrs. Wilbank's Peanut Butter Cookies

$1\frac{1}{2}$ cups shortening
$1\frac{1}{2}$ cups peanut butter
3 cups sugar
$4\frac{1}{2}$ cups all-purpose flour
$1\frac{1}{2}$ teaspoons baking soda
$1\frac{1}{2}$ teaspoons salt
$1\frac{1}{2}$ teaspoons vanilla extract
$1/3$ cup boiling water

Cream the shortening, peanut butter and sugar in a mixing bowl until light and fluffy. Stir in the flour, baking soda, salt and vanilla. Add the boiling water and mix well. Shape into walnut-size balls and arrange on a nonstick cookie sheet. Flatten with a fork, making a crisscross pattern. Bake at 350 degrees for 15 minutes.

Makes 5 dozen

Mrs. Wilbank made these cookies for many years using subsidized peanut butter and served them in the Sparkman Lunchroom. These cookies are out-of-this-world!

"Kadooze" Cookies

24 ounces chunky peanut butter
6 eggs, lightly beaten
1 cup (2 sticks) margarine, softened
1 (1-pound) package dark brown sugar
2 cups granulated sugar
4 teaspoons baking soda
1½ teaspoons vanilla extract
9 cups instant oats
4 cups (24 ounces) semisweet chocolate chips
1 (14-ounce) package M&M's candies

Combine the peanut butter, eggs, margarine, brown sugar, granulated sugar, baking soda and vanilla in a mixing bowl and mix well. Stir in the oats, chocolate chips and candies. Divide the dough into ⅓ cup portions. Shape each portion into a lemon-size ball. Arrange on a nonstick cookie sheet and flatten slightly. Bake at 350 degrees for 12 to 15 minutes.

Makes 4 dozen

Sarge at Large: *One thing for which Sarge is noted is the good behavior of her traveling students. At the end of a long trip to Orlando, the concert choir stopped at a well-known eating establishment for dinner. As Sarge was paying, the manager commented on the excellent manners of her students. Bursting with pride, Sarge made the announcement on the bus, "Ka-dooze to you for good behavior!" Who needs kudos when a good* "ka-dooze" *will do.*

Decadent White Chocolate Cranberry Nut Cookies

1 cup (2 sticks) butter, softened
1/4 cup vegetable oil
3/4 cup granulated sugar
3/4 cup packed light brown sugar
2 eggs
2 1/4 cups self-rising flour
1 1/2 teaspoons vanilla extract
2 cups (12 ounces) white chocolate chips
   or white chocolate chunks
1 (8-ounce) package dried cranberries
1 cup chopped toasted pecans or walnuts

Combine the butter, oil, granulated sugar, brown sugar, eggs, flour and vanilla in a bowl and mix well. Stir in the white chocolate chips, cranberries and pecans. Drop by heaping teaspoonfuls onto an ungreased cookie sheet. Bake at 350 degrees for 10 minutes or until light brown. Do not overbake. Add 1/2 cup sour cream for softer cookies.

Makes 3 dozen

Texas Spread Chocolate Chip Cookies

3 1/2 cups all-purpose flour
2 teaspoons salt
2 teaspoons baking soda
2 cups (4 sticks) unsalted butter, softened
3 cups packed light brown sugar
1 cup granulated sugar
4 eggs
2 teaspoons vanilla extract
1 1/2 cups (9 ounces) chocolate chips

Mix the flour, salt and baking soda together. Cream the butter, brown sugar and granulated sugar in a mixing bowl until light and fluffy. Beat in the eggs and vanilla. Add the dry ingredients gradually, beating well after each addition. Stir in the chocolate chips. Drop 2 to 3 tablespoonfuls 2 inches apart onto a nonstick cookie sheet. Bake for 8 to 10 minutes or until golden brown. Cool on a wire rack.

Makes 50

Black Tie Mocha Slices

1 tablespoon instant coffee granules
1 teaspoon hot water
3 cups all-purpose flour
1/2 teaspoon baking soda
1/4 teaspoon salt
1/2 cup shortening
1/2 cup (1 stick) unsalted butter, softened
1 cup sugar
1 egg
1/2 cup baking cocoa
3/4 teaspoon cinnamon
2 1/4 tablespoons milk
1 1/4 teaspoons vanilla extract
1/4 cup shortening
2 cups (12 ounces) milk chocolate chips
or white chocolate chips

Dissolve the coffee granules in the hot water in a bowl. Mix the flour, baking soda and salt together. Cream 1/2 cup shortening, the butter and sugar in a mixing bowl until light and fluffy. Add the coffee mixture, egg, baking cocoa, cinnamon, milk and vanilla and mix well. Add the flour mixture and mix well. Shape into two 8-inch logs and wrap tightly in plastic wrap. Chill for 6 to 24 hours. Cut the dough into 1/4-inch-thick slices and arrange on a nonstick cookie sheet. Bake at 375 degrees for 8 to 10 minutes or until light brown. Let stand until cool.

Place 1/4 cup shortening and the chocolate chips in the top of a double boiler over simmering water. Cook just until the chocolate is melted and the mixture is smooth, stirring frequently. Dip the cookies in the chocolate mixture, coating one-half of each cookie. Place on waxed paper and let stand until the chocolate is set. The cookies may be drizzled with the chocolate instead.

Makes 8 dozen

Gretel's Gingerbread Squares

$3/4$ cup ($1\frac{1}{2}$ sticks) margarine
$1/4$ cup molasses
2 cups all-purpose flour
1 cup sugar
2 teaspoons baking soda
1 teaspoon cinnamon
$1/2$ teaspoon ground cloves
$1/2$ teaspoon ginger
$1/2$ teaspoon salt
2 tablespoons sugar

Melt the margarine in a large saucepan. Let stand for 5 minutes. Add the molasses, flour, 1 cup sugar, the baking soda, cinnamon, cloves, ginger and salt and mix well. The mixture will be very thick. Press over the bottom of a 10×15-inch rimmed baking sheet sprayed with nonstick cooking spray. Sprinkle with 2 tablespoons sugar. Bake at 375 degrees for 10 to 12 minutes. Do not overbake. Cool on the baking sheet for 5 minutes. Cut into squares.

Makes 4 dozen

Syltkakor Danish Bars

$2\frac{1}{2}$ cups sifted all-purpose flour
$1/2$ cup granulated sugar
1 cup (2 sticks) cold butter, chopped
$1/3$ cup firm raspberry jam or
raspberry preserves
$1/2$ cup confectioners' sugar
1 tablespoon water

Combine the flour and granulated sugar in a bowl. Rub the butter into the dry ingredients by hand until crumbly. Knead until a soft dough forms. Shape into three 16-inch logs and place on a baking sheet. Flatten and make a slight indentation down the center of each log. Fill the indentations with the jam. Bake at 350 degrees for 15 to 18 minutes or until the edges are light brown. Mix the confectioners' sugar and water in a bowl until smooth. Spread over the logs. Cool for 15 minutes. Slice into 1-inch diagonal pieces.

Makes 2 dozen

Goo-Gooey Bars

2 cups (12 ounces) semisweet chocolate chips
1 (14-ounce) can sweetened condensed milk
2 tablespoons butter
2 cups unsalted dry-roasted peanuts
1 (10-ounce) package miniature marshmallows

Combine the chocolate chips, condensed milk and butter in a saucepan. Cook over low heat until the chocolate chips are melted and the mixture is smooth, stirring fequently. Stir in the peanuts and marshmallows, coating well with the chocolate mixture. Pour into a 9×13-inch baking pan lined with waxed paper. Chill until set. Remove from the pan and peel off the waxed paper. Cut into bars.

Makes 30 to 35

Pecan Pralines

1½ cups granulated sugar
¾ cup packed brown sugar
½ cup evaporated milk
6 tablespoons butter
2 cups pecans, toasted
1 tablespoon vanilla extract

Mix the granulated sugar, brown sugar, evaporated milk, butter, pecans and vanilla in a saucepan. Cook to 234 to 240 degrees on a candy thermometer, soft ball stage, stirring constantly. Remove from the heat and stir constantly until the mixture thickens and the pecans rise to the top. Drop by spoonfuls onto buttered waxed paper. Let stand until cool.

Makes 3 dozen

Blistering Brittle

$1\frac{1}{2}$ teaspoons hot red pepper sauce
$\frac{1}{4}$ teaspoon ground allspice
$1\frac{1}{4}$ cups dry-roasted peanuts
1 cup sugar
$\frac{1}{2}$ cup light corn syrup
1 teaspoon butter
1 teaspoon vanilla extract
$1\frac{1}{2}$ teaspoons baking soda

Mix the hot sauce and allspice in a bowl. Add the peanuts and toss to coat. Mix the sugar and corn syrup in a microwave-safe bowl. Microwave on High for 4 minutes; mix well. Stir in the peanuts. Microwave for 5 minutes or until light brown. Stir in the butter and vanilla. Microwave for 30 to 60 seconds. Add the baking soda and stir gently until the mixture is foamy. Pour onto a large baking sheet sprayed with nonstick cooking spray. Stretch into a thin layer by pulling the mixture with two forks. Cool until firm. Break into pieces.

Makes 1 pound

Almond Roca

1 cup (2 sticks) butter
1 cup (2 sticks) margarine
3 cups sugar
2 king-size chocolate candy bars, shaved
$1\frac{1}{2}$ cups almonds with skins, toasted and chopped

Melt the butter and margarine in a saucepan. Stir in the sugar. Cook to 300 degrees on a candy thermometer. Pour onto a rimmed baking sheet. Sprinkle with the chocolate immediately. Let stand for several minutes. Spread the almonds over the chocolate. Let stand until cool. Cut into small bars. May substitute pecans for the almonds.

Makes 10 dozen

Chopping chocolate can be a mess. Use a serrated knife—the teeth of the knife grab the chocolate without scattering it all over the kitchen.

French Silk Chocolate Pie

2 egg whites
1/8 teaspoon cream of tartar
1/8 teaspoon salt
1/2 cup sugar
1/2 cup chopped pecans
1/2 teaspoon vanilla extract
1/2 cup (1 stick) butter, softened
3/4 cup sugar
1 ounce unsweetened chocolate, melted
2 eggs
1/2 teaspoon vanilla extract
Salt to taste
1 cup heavy whipping cream, whipped

Combine the egg whites, cream of tartar and 1/8 teaspoon salt in a mixing bowl. Beat until foamy. Add 1/2 cup sugar 2 tablespoons at a time, beating constantly until stiff peaks form. Fold in the pecans and 1/2 teaspoon vanilla. Spread over the bottom and up the side of a lightly greased 8-inch pie plate, building the edge 1/2 inch above the pie plate. Bake at 300 degrees for 50 to 55 minutes or until light brown. Cool on a wire rack.

Cream the butter in a mixing bowl. Add 3/4 cup sugar gradually, mixing well after each addition. Stir in the chocolate. Add the eggs one at a time, mixing for 4 to 5 minutes after each addition. Stir in 1/2 teaspoon vanilla and salt to taste. Pour into the meringue shell. Chill until serving time. Serve with the whipped cream.

If you are concerned about using raw eggs, use eggs pasteurized in their shells, which are available at some specialty food stores, or use equivalent amounts of pasteurized egg substitute and meringue powder and follow the package directions.

Serves 6

White Chocolate Key Lime Pie

11 ounces white chocolate chips
1 cup whipping cream
1 tablespoon sour cream
1/3 cup fresh Key lime juice
1 teaspoon grated lime zest
1/2 teaspoon vanilla extract
1 baked (9-inch) pie shell

Combine the white chocolate chips and cream in a saucepan. Cook over low heat for 5 minutes or until the white chocolate is melted and the mixture is smooth, stirring constantly. Remove from the heat and stir in the sour cream, lime juice, lime zest and vanilla. Pour into the pie shell. Chill, covered, for 8 hours. Garnish with freshly whipped cream and lime slices.

Serves 8

Peach Pie

1/2 cup (1 stick) butter, softened
1 cup sugar
3 egg yolks
2 tablespoons all-purpose flour
2 cups sliced peaches
1 unbaked (9-inch) pie shell
3 egg whites
6 tablespoons sugar
1/2 teaspoon vanilla extract

Cream the butter and 1 cup sugar in a mixing bowl until light and fluffy. Add the egg yolks one at a time, mixing well after each addition. Stir in the flour. Fold in the peaches. Pour into the pie shell. Bake at 325 degrees for 1 hour. Beat the egg whites in a mixing bowl until soft peaks form. Add 6 tablespoons sugar 1 tablespoon at a time, beating constantly at high speed until stiff peaks form. Beat in the vanilla. Top the hot pie with the meringue, sealing to the edge. Bake until the meringue is light brown.

Serves 8

Japanese Fruit Pie

2 egg whites
1/2 cup (1 stick) butter, softened
1 cup sugar
2 egg yolks
1/2 cup raisins
1/2 cup chopped pecans
1/2 cup shredded coconut
1 cup all-purpose flour
1/2 teaspoon salt
1/3 cup shortening
1 egg, lightly beaten
1 teaspoon lemon juice

Beat the egg whites in a mixing bowl until stiff peaks form; set aside. Cream the butter, sugar and egg yolks in a mixing bowl until light and fluffy. Stir in the raisins, pecans and coconut. Fold in the beaten egg whites.

Combine the flour and salt in a bowl. Cut in the shortening until crumbly. Add the egg and lemon juice and mix until the dough holds together. Roll out the dough and fit into a pie plate. Pour the filling into the pastry-lined pie plate. Bake at 300 degrees for 1 hour or until the filling is set.

Serves 8

Maxine's Champion Cherry Pie

2 1/2 cups drained canned tart cherries
1/4 cup cherry juice
1 cup sugar
3 tablespoons all-purpose flour
1/4 teaspoon salt
1/4 teaspoon red food coloring
1/8 teaspoon almond extract
2 cups sifted all-purpose flour
1 tablespoon sugar
1 teaspoon salt
2/3 cup shortening
1/3 cup cold milk
2 tablespoons butter

Combine the cherries, cherry juice, 1 cup sugar, 3 tablespoons flour, 1/4 teaspoon salt, the food coloring and almond extract in a bowl. Stir gently to mix; set aside.

Combine 2 cups sifted flour, 1 tablespoon sugar and 1 teaspoon salt in a bowl. Cut in the shortening until crumbly. Add the milk 1 tablespoon at a time, stirring constantly until the dough holds together. Divide the dough into halves. Roll one-half of the dough into a 12-inch circle on a lightly floured surface. Fit into an 8- or 9-inch pie plate. Melt 1 tablespoon of the butter. Brush over the edge of the pie shell.

Spoon the cherry mixture into the pastry-lined pie plate. Dot with the remaining 1 tablespoon butter. Roll the remaining pastry on a lightly floured surface and cut into strips. Arrange lattice-fashion over the pie. Bake at 450 degrees for 5 minutes. Reduce the oven temperature to 375 degrees. Bake for 30 to 35 minutes or until golden brown. Cover the edge with foil if the edge begins to get too brown.

Serves 6 to 8

In February 1953, Butler High School student Maxine Walker won the National Cherry Pie Baking Contest. She traveled to Washington, D.C., where she baked a cherry pie for First Lady Mamie Eisenhower. She gave the First Lady an autographed recipe for her award-winning pie. Maxine won an all-expense paid trip to Washington, D.C., and New York City. Her prizes also included a new stove and $100 in cash. On March 5th she was honored by a motorcade viewed by twelve thousand people in Huntsville, and two hundred people attended a banquet in her honor at the Russel Erskine Hotel where she received checks from local merchants. Maxine Walker Patrick continues to reside in the Huntsville area and still bakes the best cherry pie in town. We are privileged to have this coveted recipe in our book.

Contributors

Pam Alford
Martha Allen
Shirley Allen
Nell Anderson
Laura Ayers
Sue Bailey
Susan Wilkerson Bailey
Tarrill E. Barnett
Frances Barry
LaNette Bass
Sandra J. Barrett Beckett
Anissa R. Benson
Vicki Blackwood
Diana Jones Brooks
Martha Allen Brooks
Mary Gail Wallace Broussard
Eulah Brown
Amy Champion Bryan
Brea Anna Burton
Carmelita Burton
Melanie Busby
Andrea Carey
Joan Carey
Kathryne Channell
Mary Jo Chaudoin
Bama Folsom Chesser
Madelyn Jamelle Chesser
Mary Chunn
Vicki Chunn
Ann Clark
Deborah C. Clay
Kim Clouser
Andrea Converse
Regina Cook
Angie Cornelius
Reese Covington
Ginny Cox
Frances Crockett
Cheryl Cunningham
Kim Davis
Sherrye Davis
Rhonda Dennison
Leslie DeVore
Stephanie DeVore
Teresa DeVore
Rhonda Dickens
Wendy Diffey
Kenny Dodson
Angela Drensek
Marvelee Durham
Tracy Dyess
Susan Earp
Doris Eby
Joan Edminson
Juanita Edmondson
Dena Einhorn
Bonnelle Hill Elkins
Janet England
Ronita England
Virginia Erwin
Sharron Evars
Chris Plitt Farber
Beth Flatt
Linda Lou Foster
Jo Frazier
Mrs. Raymond Fuller
Mary Katherine Gaffin
Teresa Gaffin
Katherine Garrison
Linda Goode
Tami Grant
Lisa Graveman
Sandra Gray
Wendy Green
Glenna Hadley
Ginger Hamlett
Paula Hamlett
Sera Hamlett
Monica Hammond
Bettye Hamric
Holly Beth Hamric
Lane Hamric
Mindy Hamric
Anita Quandt Hand
Cara Hargett
Erika Harless
Margaret Lindi Heffington
Suzanne Heffington
Henri Jo McDaniel Helstowski
Silvia C. Henderson
Amy Brown Hendrixson
Jean Hindman
Joy Ragland Hogan
Charlotte T. Homan
Ann Hopkins
Doris Hosse
Becky Houbregs
Faye Hubbard
Becky Hughes
Pat Huntley
Alice Ivey
Bennie Jacks
Kristy Jacks
Lou Anne Maples Jackson
Dana Jefferson
Alice Johnson
Cindy Johnston
Garland Johnston
Geal T. Jones
Jean Jones
Libby Jones
Linda Jones
Elaine Jordan
Betty Jean Keenum
Tara Dillard Kelly
Betty Kemp
Faye Khodanian
Cookie Kimbrough
Dara Kimbrough
Kara Kimbrough
Martha Kimbrough
Noah Kimbrough
Kathleen Laeupple
Pat Morrison Laney
Cynthia Sibley Lau
Nancy Lemmons
Karen Lindsey
Nell Long
Karen Lowery
Mary Ann Lowery
Linda Lyons
Madison Academy Cafeteria

Rada Malone
Isabel Maltman
Johnna Mann
Margaret Mann
Mable Maples
Dot Massey
Irene Mathis
Julie Mathis
Sonja Mathis
Brenda Matthews
Lisa Mayes
Doris McCafferty
Lisa McCrary
Melissa McCutcheon
Henri McDaniel
Jill McMurthrie
Kim Medlen
Becky Mercer
Connie Mercer
Mary Milam
Mary Margaret Miller
Melissa Milo
Carol Milton
Ann Minor
Kim Minor
Rita Mitchell
Teri Mitchell
Trudy Moore
Carolyn Moorhead
Carolyn E. Moses
Joan Moss
Joan Nahay
Mary Etta Neiland
Robbie Norman
Kim Dant Oliver
Judith Outlaw
Jan Parker
Opal P. Parker
Lynn Parrish
Maxine Walker Patrick
Kathy Passon
Sue Passon
Jim (Papa) Phillips
Julia Phillips

Virginia Hancock Phillips
Wendi Pollard
Raneé Pruitt
Cindy Moore Richardson
Katheryn Richter
Cindy Rieder
Joyce Rodgers
Connie Rogers
Leanne Rogers
Rhonda Smith Ross
Darlene Routon
Christina G. Russell
Milla Sachs
Freida Sadler
Molly Sadler
Cindy Saylor
Gloria Tucker Scherzinger
Tasha K. Schors
Donna Schrader
Sallie Scott
Tami Segrest
Clis Shates
Mrs. Henry M. Shuey
Evelyn Sissom
Pat Sisson
Mildred Smelser
Diane Smith
Jane Smith
Margie Swafford Smith
Mary Anne Smith
Rachel Smith
Carol Sockwell
Anna Standridge
Shirley Stansbury
Mary Beth Stewart
Sara Strickland
Lottie Swafford
Shea Burton Swindle
Carol Sibley Taylor
Lyle Theisen
Pat Theisen
Karen Sims Thomas
Melissa Ford Thornton
Kim Thrasher

Nancy Dee Tipton
Roslynn Tomlinson
Mary Toney
Robbie Tribble
Christy Troxell
Kayla Troxell
Megan Tucker
Ruby Tucker
Deanna Tuten
Lauren Tuten
Marian Tuten
Teresa Tuten
Suzanne VanDyke
Sharon Vaughn
Christy Vernon
Carol Wardlaw
Tonya Ware
Carolyn Watson
Barbara Webster
Jeanne S. Westrope
Dianne Whitaker
Kim Whitaker
Michelle White
Donna Wicks
Jean Wilcoxson
Mary Alice Wilhelm
Donna Wilkerson
Gloria Wilkerson
Norma Williams
Jamie Willis
Lynne Woods
Janet Yeager
Lisa Yokley

Index

Order information

FROM COTTON TO COUNTDOWN

A CULINARY CELEBRATION OF SOUTHERN TRADITION

Ladies Association
of Madison Academy
325 Slaughter Road
Madison, Alabama 35758

256-971-1619
www.macademy.org